# Using Microcomputers
# in Social Science Research

# Using Microcomputers in Social Science Research

Mark D. Shermis
Paul M. Stemmer, Jr.
Carl F. Berger
G. Ernest Anderson, Jr.

**Allyn and Bacon**
Boston   London   Toronto   Sydney   Tokyo   Singapore

Aquisitions editor: Carol Wada
Editorial/production supervision: Evalyn Schoppet
Cover design: Diane Conner
Manufacturing buyer: MaryAnn Gloriande
Prepress buyer: Debbie Kesar

**Library of Congress Cataloging-in-Publication Data**

Using microcomputers in social science research / Mark D. Shermis . . .
  [et al.]
      p.    cm.
    Includes bibliographical references and index.
    ISBN 0–13–933573–0
    1.  Social sciences—Data processing.   2.  Microcomputers.
  I. Shermis, Mark D.
  H61.3.U85   1991
  300′ .285′5416—dc20                                                    90–27579
                                                                         CIP

ISBN 0-13-933573-0

Printed in the United States of America
10  9  8  7  6  5  4  3  2  1    96  95  94  93  92  91

To our wives,
Sue, Karen, Shari, and Patricia
whose patience and understanding made this book possible.

# Contents

## 2 Beginning the Research    15

## 3 Planning the Research: Administrative    37

## 4 Planning the Research: Operational    65

## 5 Data Collection    87

# 6  Analyzing Results      109

# 7  Disseminating the Results      143

8   Perils, Pitfalls, and Promises     167

# Preface

Like it or not, you are a participant in a revolution. Although the thought may bring to mind images of burning villages and thundering cannons, this revolution is much less obvious than that. It is no less dramatic, however. The information revolution, in which the microcomputer is playing a major role, is having far-reaching effects on the way research is conducted. This book is intended to introduce you to the ways the microcomputer is revolutionizing social science research, and to give you guidance in putting this marvelous tool to work for you.

Each of us is an active researcher who became interested in microcomputers when they first became commercially available in the late 1970s. At that time microcomputers were expensive, slow, and of limited capacity in comparison to the larger, more traditional computers, yet we were fascinated by the freedom that they provided. At first our fellow researchers couldn't understand why we spent so much time learning operating systems, programming languages, and troubleshooting and debugging techniques, especially when they could accomplish research tasks so much more easily with larger computers.

Ten years later, we are still using very much the same applications, but now the software is far more sophisticated and the power, speed, and capacity of the microcomputer have increased a thousandfold. For example, author Carl Berger's first data-analysis package was self-programmed, required a tape recorder for program input, and was executed on a 16K (16,000 bytes of memory) PET microcomputer. Carl would start a regression analysis, go to bed, and wake up the next morning to see if it was finished. A regression analysis on the university's mainframe would have been performed in less than a second! Today Carl uses a five-megabyte machine (five million bytes of memory) and calculates his statistics on a professionally developed analysis package. The regression analysis that took all night to run ten years earlier now takes just a few seconds. Although the task still takes longer to run on his microcomputer than it would take on a mainframe, when you consider the steps required to establish mainframe communications, transmit and edit data, and get the results back, the elapsed time for most small and medium-sized jobs actually is less.

We still use the mainframe for large analyses, centralized database management, and electronic mail, but the microcomputer, because of its ease of use and general availability, clearly has changed the way we conduct research. And our formerly skeptical colleagues now come to us for advice on what software and hardware to purchase and how to us it.

An all-purpose tool usually becomes very popular very quickly, and the microcomputer has proven to be no exception. In 1977, 50,000 computers were being built per year around the world. By 1987, 50,000 computers were being built *per day* (Sculley, 1988). The pace of development in the field of computer support for social science research has been equally breathtaking. Since we began giving workshops in 1981 on the microcomputer in social science research, the field has grown so fast that each year we've had to add totally new areas of computer support. The microcomputer is not only greatly enhancing the power of the researcher, it is also opening up new avenues and methods of research.

Whether you are considering the purchase of a microcomputer or have just bought one, or you want to expand on your system to accomplish multiple tasks, this book can help you. In it we describe ways of using microcomputers in social science research settings. We have found the microcomputer to be a virtually universal tool, the power of which lies in its ability to integrate and "informate" (Zuboff, 1986) the entire research process. While our emphasis is on software applications, we occasionally mention hardware components that we think you may find useful. Our examples illustrate specific packages for either Apple Macintosh or PC systems; usually the same or very similar software is available for both. We have tried our best to be machine-independent.

We expect the concepts presented here to remain relatively stable over time. The software illustrated is changing at an accelerated pace, and what looks good today may become obsolete very quickly as newer, better offerings become available. Yet future innovations will only serve to facilitate the kinds of techniques we are demonstrating and encouraging you to try.

We have designed this book for the intermediate to advanced researcher who has some basic knowledge of the microcomputer. An excellent introduction to microcomputers in research can be found in Craig Johnson (1983), *Microcomputers in Educational Research*, or Madron et al. (1985), *Using Microcomputers in Research.*

The book is intended to provide a broad overview of the microcomputer's multifaceted role in the research process. Since we're aiming for a broad overview, we cannot cover all the details of specific research techniques, nor can we go into minute detail about how to use specific software or applications. Where appropriate, we will suggest more specialized publications that offer more explanation. By sharing the "big picture" as we see it, we hope to show how useful the microcomputer can be. The more integrated its use, the more productive and efficient the researcher becomes.

M.S.
P.S.
C.B.
E. A.

# Credits and Copyrights

# 1

# Managing Complexity

## ENTERING THE "BIT STREAM"

The "bit stream" is a convenient way to describe the flow of information around us and that part we personally manage. The microcomputer has become a ubiquitous tool for tapping into and managing the stream of information that inundates us.

There are many ways to enter the "bit stream." Authors Mark Shermis and Paul Stemmer became involved with microcomputers because they were looking for ways to cut down on dissertation costs. They figured they would save money by typing their own work and by performing their own analyses at home. It didn't turn out that way, but they didn't mind. Their new-found interest soon became an addiction, and they found themselves becoming more and more involved with microcomputers.

Actually, Mark and Paul's initial use of microcomputers is typical of how most people become involved with them—they purchase a microcomputer for one primary task, such as word processing or database management, but soon find that it is a very versatile device capable of many other uses. The variety of software offerings make the microcomputer a chameleon-like tool, and thus it can represent different things to different people.

Author Ernie Anderson was seeking a way to bring the interactive capability of the computer to his research and statistics courses. He regularly uses the computer to demonstrate and then, through hands-on practice, reinforce the basic concepts of data analysis. Carl Berger was looking at microcomputers as a vehicle to stimulate his students to become more involved in science education and to increase the productivity of his own lines of scholarship.

The computerization of some research tasks is not new. For some years, researchers have used sophisticated statistical packages to analyze their data. More recently, many mainframe computing systems have added graphics capabilities that contribute to the effective display of data. As we will soon see, however, the analysis and dissemination steps of the research cycle, while important, are just two of the many stages researchers must traverse in pursuit of systematic inquiry.

The microcomputer also has taught its "big brother," the mainframe, some manners. Many researchers, recalling the pain of learning a difficult mainframe package, are somewhat reticent about learning microcomputer packages. However, microcomputer packages are far more friendly than mainframe packages, and by using various software packages to integrate the steps of the research process, the researcher can achieve an exceedingly high level of efficiency.


## A BRIEF HISTORY

Books on the history of the computer abound. The reader is referred to *The Computer Challenge* by Hussain and Hussain (1986) for a detailed study. Here we provide but a brief overview.

Engineers have developed four generations of computers and are on the brink of launching the fifth. Each generation of computers has been exponentially improved in power, speed, and ease of operation. For a better understanding of how rapid advances have been, consider the following analogy: if the advances in the automobile industry had matched those in the computer industry, a present-day Rolls Royce would cost $2.50 and get about 2 million miles per gallon. The bad news is that the car would be the size of a thimble.


### The Birth of Automation—The Turn of the Century

In a sense, we can say that the computer actually owes its orgins to the need to conduct social research. Herman Hollerith, an American inventor, developed a punch-card system for processing the 1890 U.S. census data. He managed to reduce the time necessary to tabulate the census from $7\frac{1}{2}$ years to less than six months. Keep in mind that the mechanical Hollerith card reader, the calculator, and the typewriter were produced during the industrial revolution and were improved considerably over the ensuing years. During the information revolution, the electronic computer integrated all three of these devices and many more.

### The Embryonic Stage—The 1930s and 1940s

The embryonic stage of the modern electronic computer began in the late 1930s and early 1940s (see Figure 1.1*). At that time, John Atanasoff and Clifford Berry of Iowa State University developed the first electronic machine to solve linear equations; it was known as the "ABC." Howard Aiken at Harvard University, with the help of IBM, developed what was the first widely known sequence-controlled calculator ("computer"), the Mark I. It was controlled by punched tape that was fed through a reader via a series of pulleys.[†] World War II spurred the development of the ENIAC (Electronic Numerical Integrator and Calculator), a thousand times faster than the Mark I. Designed to calculate ballistic trajectories, the Mark I was produced in 1943 but remained a secret project until 1955.

### The First Generation—The 1950s

The first commercial computer, the UNIVAC, was released in 1951. Using a special machine language for programming, it could execute 1000 instructions per second (today an IBM PS/2 Model 80 or a Mac II can execute about 25,000 instructions per second). The UNIVAC had a memory capacity of 10,000 to 20,000 characters (compared to a capacity of 16 million for today's IBM PS/2 Model 80 or Mac II), and used vacuum tubes that failed after every few hours of operation.

### The Second Generation—The 1960s

The computers of the 1960s were a thousand times faster than the UNIVAC, used cards similar to Hollerith's for input (a "batch" of cards gave it the name "batch mode"), and were about a hundred to a

---

*Adapted from Daniel C. Atkins, Dean, College of Engineering, The University of Michigan.
[†]This is the derivation of the computer slang word "loop."

FIGURE 1.1. Development of Computers Over the Last Five
Decades

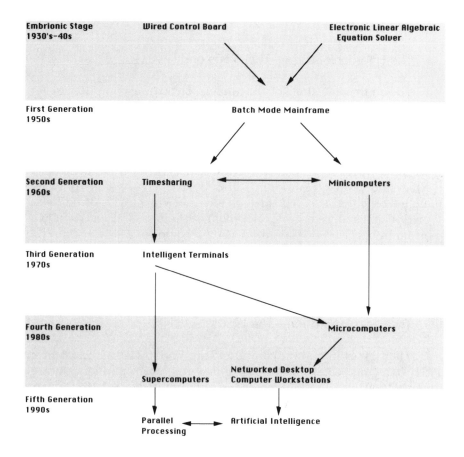

thousand times more reliable due to the invention of the transistor. They used high-level programming languages such as FORTRAN (FORmula TRANslator) and COBOL (COmmon Business Oriented Language), which facilitated the development of database systems and advanced their use in science (and no doubt launched the acronym race). In the early 1960s, researchers at UCLA used FORTRAN to develop the BMD (BioMeD) statistical packages. By the mid-1960s SPSS (Statistical Packages for the Social Sciences) was in development, and soon after that the SAS (Statistical Analysis System), written in PL/1 (Programming Language/1).

The operating systems of the 1960s computers were noninteractive and therefore have been dubbed "batch mode mainframes." However, they did allow knowledgeable and dedicated researchers to run software that made their jobs easier.

### The Third Generation—The 1970s

By the 1970s, integrated circuitry had speeded up the computer by a factor of 100,000 and increased reliability a million times over the first generation. This power permitted timesharing—input and output could be routed to a terminal instead of being submitted on cards and printed on a printer.

Digital Equipment Corporation (DEC) and others began to develop smaller, less expensive computers, dubbed minicomputers, which employed timesharing techniques but for fewer simultaneous users. Typically, they could accommodate from 5 to 50 terminals (today some minicomputers can host an almost unlimited number of terminals). The smaller size and lower cost of these computers enabled them to find their niche in decentralized processing. Statistical packages such as BMD, SPSS, and SAS were transferred to these smaller machines. Timesharing systems were used to make the packages more attractive, and sophisticated graphics were added to make the packages more useful. Their cost effectiveness led users to put them to tasks other than scientific or database processing, such as text processing (the use of the computer to generate manuscripts).

The development of faster, more powerful mainframes also continued during this period. Toward the end of the 1970s, intelligent terminals became popular. These devices enabled extensive editing to be done quickly on the terminal, then sent to the mainframe for rapid alteration of the file without the mainframe having to acknowledge each change. In addition, the "conversation"—electronic transactions between the user and the computer—could be saved and paged backwards as well as forwards so that the user could trace what had transpired.

### The Fourth Generation—The 1980s

The use of LSI and VLSI (Large Scale Integrated and Very Large Scale Integrated) circuits led to the development of a microprocessor on a single chip. The capacity to put most of the circuitry of a computer on one silicon chip enabled the development of a microcomputer—by two college dropouts, Steve Wosniak and Steve

Jobs*—with the same power as many third-generation mainframe computers, and led the way to the current generation of micros.

During the 1980s the cost effectiveness of microcomputers increased a hundredfold. The result has been steady advancements in word processing—and, more recently, desktop publishing, whereby text and graphics can be printed at near-typeset quality—and other desktop computing applications. The fact that we can customize the microcomputer's operating system and rely on its graphics and local control means that microcomputer applications, including statistical analysis packages, no longer need to be tied to the descendants of card readers, so applications are much easier to learn and use. Graphics can be displayed on high-resolution screens and printed without highly sophisticated equipment.

The supercomputer of the early 1980s, which increased in calculation power by a factor of one hundred within a single generation, was developed by the brilliant computer architect Seymour Cray. To date, the expense of supercomputers has limited their use to military, nuclear, weather, and scientific research. However, assuming that computation costs will continue to decline, it should not be long before social scientists have access to these machines. Moreover, supercomputers are now being used to design the next generation of personal microcomputers.[†]

In this book we focus on the microcomputer, but as Figure 1.1 shows, we have not ignored mini- and mainframe computers, for we continue to depend on these larger systems to provide the backbone of support in what is known as distributed processing. Each machine—the micro-, mini-, mainframe, or supercomputer—has an important role in the support of research. We have noticed, however, that our use of microcomputers continues to increase while our use of the mainframe declines.

It is essentially a matter of choosing the right tool for the job. When these various machines are used effectively for what they do best, they form a symbiotic network that benefits the user. The stage in which we find ourselves now is that of the networked desktop-computer workstation. That is, high-powered personal computers can now access and share information with mainframes, minicomputers, and supercomputers when the power requirements of the particular application call for it (word processing on a supercomputer would be like killing a fly with a howitzer). One network providing

---

*Wozniak has since graduated from the University of California, Berkeley, with a degree in cognitive science and teacher education.

[†]However, rumor has it that Seymour Cray is designing part of his next generation of supercomputers with a Macintosh II microcomputer.

distributed processing is the National Science Foundation Network (NSFNET), which is supported by a grant from the National Science Foundation, IBM, and MCI and housed at the University of Michigan. NSFNET ties together campus and scientific networks all over the country, offering users access to at least three supercomputers and hundreds of mainframes and minicomputers.

### The Fifth Generation—The 1990s

It is always difficult to look ahead in such a speculative area as this. The fifth generation of computers will be exciting; that much is guaranteed. Hardware advances, designed with Very, Very Large Scale Integrated (VVLSI) circuits, will give us the power and capacity for parallel processing (the same form the human brain uses) and artificial intelligence (the ability of the computer to think about its actions and to work on problems independently).

One futuristic experiment is Rex, under development at AT&T Bell Laboratories. Rex is a data-analysis package that assists and advises the researcher in properly analyzing a set of data. Rex does what the user commands, but cleverly (and, one hopes, tactfully) makes suggestions to the user about appropriate analysis. For example, the user might request, in written English, a $t$-test on two groups. Rex would alert the user that the distribution of the scores is highly skewed; it might question the appropriateness of a $t$-test and suggest a nonparametric statistic as an alternative. Rex is designed to be an advisor, not a dictator, so the user can tell Rex to proceed with the $t$-test analysis anyway (researchers who are also consultants will be familiar with this situation). Employed properly, artificial intelligence programs such as Rex can be immensely useful to the researcher. Decision-support systems, data analysis systems, and hypermedia (nonlinear branching databases that incorporate written, aural, and visual materials), combined with artificial intelligence, may sound revolutionary from where we are today, but are just on the horizon.

## THE NATURE OF RESEARCH: PROBLEM SOLVING

Figure 1.2 illustrates the ten steps in the research cycle,* which we present as a model of the activities in which researchers typically en-

*Adapted from Terrence Davidson, Ph.D., School of Education, The University of Michigan.

## FIGURE 1.2.  The Research Cycle

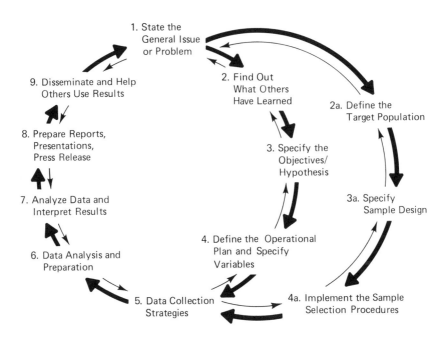

gage, independent of the methods they employ to collect data. The reader is invited to explore the many different steps of research described in a variety of other handbooks and texts (cf. Borg & Gall, 1989).

First, note that there is no single starting place in the research cycle. A study can begin anywhere. However, generally the researcher begins by defining a problem of interest and then proceeds clockwise around the cycle. The study culminates with the dissemination of the research findings. The smaller arrows proceeding counterclockwise remind us that we cannot always progress in a forward direction. Sometimes working through a step uncovers flaws in our thinking at a previous step, in which case we must retrace our steps and correct our thinking before proceeding forward (clockwise) once again. (You will note that with this model we have been able to capture the famous "one step forward, three steps back" theory.) In the following discussion, once we have demonstrated each of the activities common to a typical research study, we show how the computer can intervene in these activities in such a way as to improve their efficiency and raise the quality of the results.

Most researchers begin with a statement of general purpose

(Step 1). This statement articulates why the research is being conducted and what benefits are anticipated from studying the problem. A review of the previous research (Step 2) delineates what others know about the problem. Clarification of the problem will allow us to specify formal objectives or hypotheses (Step 3). The specification of objectives or hypotheses prods the researcher to identify variables (Step 4) in measurable ways. For example, one conceptual definition of intelligence is "an organism's ability to successfully adapt to its environment." Given this definition, a cockroach may be thought of as "intelligent." By contrast, the operational definition of intelligence as the score derived from an intelligence test may restrict its overall validity, but certainly defines the construct in a clearly replicable way. We begin to see already how this cycle may force us to work backwards, as we discover from previous research that a definition is too vague or that the constructs we propose to study are unresearchable.

While many variables are self-evident (e.g., gender), more complex variables must be combined in an operational definition (e.g., socio-economic status). In a simple survey, the development of a cohesive instrument (Step 5) requires that questions (variables) be asked in logical sequence. We may also find that standardized tests, or tests which the researcher constructs, will be useful in operationalizing variables.

Most large studies make provisions for field-testing the instrument (Step 5). Field-testing generally is done in two stages. In a pretest, the researcher usually tests the efficacy of the research instruments (e.g., Is the instrument working the way it was designed to work?). In a pilot study, the researcher's task is to identify potential flaws in the administration of the study. As such, a pilot study is a sort of a "dress rehearsal" for the main study.

In conjunction with the steps just outlined, the researcher must focus on defining the target population (Step 2a), or the population of interest. The sample design (Step 3a) must facilitate appropriate generalizations from the sample to the specified target population. Moreover, properly selecting the sample requires that the researcher be able to identify potential sources of bias (Kish, 1965). We have illustrated these steps by putting them in a semicircle to the right of Steps 1–5.

If results from the pilot study merit continuance of the study, the formal administration and supervision of data collection can begin (Step 6). To ensure the reliability of the information collected, an investigator must prepare the data for analysis, usually through a process of editing and coding (Step 7). This step is designed to introduce procedures to detect and correct errors that may have been introduced inadvertently. Once a proper data set has been constructed, researchers can proceed to statistical analysis and the subsequent interpretation of that analysis (Step 8). This interpretation typically forms the basis of the investigator's report (Step 9) on how the original problem might be reformulated.

The researcher's responsibility does not end with the generation of a report. If the research has been done carefully and is useful and valid, then it is the researcher's responsibility to see that as many people as possible learn of the findings. This dissemination of information (Step 10) can take the form of articles, press releases, presentations, and conferences. If the research is successful, it should contribute in some way to our understanding of the problem under study. However, because the researcher will have been exposed to new insights, as well as better procedures, research designs, and instrumentation, additional questions usually have been raised, and the problem as it is now understood may have to be examined further. And so the research cycle begins again.

We begin to see how the computer can facilitate and support each of these researcher-initiated activities. The following brief descriptions of how the computer can help at some of the stages illustrate the concept of computer-enhanced research support. The remaining chapters detail this support at each stage.

## "INFORMATING" THE PROCESS

Shoshona Zuboff (1988), in her book *The Age of the Smart Machine*, points out that we have entered the phase of the information revolution where entirely new ways of doing and thinking are possible. Analogous to the way the industrial revolution used the term "automate" to represent the machine's taking over manual labor, "informate" refers to the automation of manual ways of dealing with information. In the process, our behavior and thinking are changed. For example, in most major grocery stores computers at the checkout counter scan the Universal Product Code (UPC) on each item and add the price of the product to the consumer's bill. The benefits of this automated checkout process are reduced labor costs for the store (Zuboff discusses the smaller labor force and lower level of skill required by staff utilizing scanning machines), more accurate bills for the consumer, reduced loss to the store through error, and faster checkouts. But there is an informating side to this process, too. The information these computers collect can track inventory going out of the store, analyze daily trends, and make stocking suggestions. Thus, the informating process adds a value and capacity that simply were not present in the old way of doing things.

The microcomputer is having the same synergistic effect on the research process. Not only can the micro facilitate the researcher's study, but side benefits may emerge as well. For example, a "template" of a research budget from one project could prove useful in planning the next project.

## A QUICK TOUR OF THE RESEARCH CYCLE
## ON THE MICROCOMPUTER

On-line computer databases such as Bibliographic Retrieval System (BRS) and DIALOG serve as a convenient and comprehensive electronic resource to assist the researcher in finding out what others know (see Step 2 on the Research Cycle in Figure 1.2). The researcher can use CD-ROM (Compact Disk—Read Only Memory) devices to search databases such as ERIC and PsyInfo. In addition, software exists in the form of personal bibliographic retrieval systems (e.g., electronic card files) to help the researcher organize information quickly and accurately. This organization will be helpful when it comes time to specify the variables (Step 4) and writing the report (Step 9).

While the specification and identification of variables in a study (Step 4) typically are the result of deliberate decisions, some variables may be introduced into a project simply because information on subjects is easily retrievable (e.g., a school district's test scores or a patient's hospital records). Additionally, the researcher must select each variable so that the collected data answer the research hypotheses (Step 3). Shermis, Cole, and Heyden (1990) have developed a computer program that takes the researcher through an algorithm for the selection of statistics and describes the characteristics of variables associated with such statistics.

If concepts are operationalized through the construction of questions (e.g., through a questionnaire or interview), word processing is a computer-related step that might be used to facilitate the presentation of questions (Step 5). Some computer programs actually facilitate the construction of the entire instrument. StatSoft, Inc., for example, has developed a computer program, called *Q-Fast*™, designed to support the construction, administration, and data reporting of survey questionnaires.

Computers also have been helpful in the sampling process (Step 3a and 4a). Some databases (e.g., DORIS) contain U.S. Census information that could be used to identify the characteristics of a target population. Shermis (1983) reviewed software designed to calculate sizes for samples obtained by simple random selection. PSRC Software has developed a program called *MaCATI*™, which can implement a Random Digit Dialing (RDD) algorithm in a telephone survey.

The pilot stage often is critical to a project's success. It is during this phase that investigators try to maximize the validity and reliability of their instruments (Step 5).

Berger, Shermis, and Stemmer (1982) distinguish between two different types of computer-mediated strategies for data collection (Step 6). The first, microcomputer-aided collection, refers to the use of the microcomputer for a task that usually is performed by hand or some other device. In the second type, called microcomputer-automated research, the microcomputer, without human intervention, performs all the steps in acquiring and coding the data. In the latter strategy, the microcomputer might provide both stimuli and responses and automatically collect, code, and store information. Newman and Berger (1984) used this technique of data collection to ascertain the types of cognitive strategies used by sixth-graders to estimate ratios. *MindLab*™, a computer program for creating, editing, and running simple psychology experiments in perception and cognition, has been developed for the Macintosh computer by Meike (1987). Figure 1.3 illustrates a typical development screen for this program.

FIGURE 1.3. Development Screen for *MindLab* 2.1.1

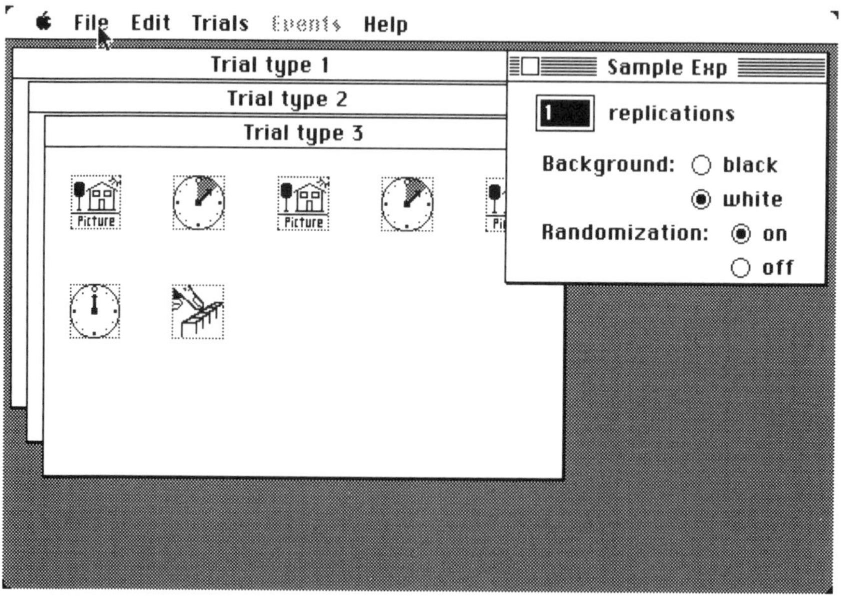

Once data have been collected, they must be prepared for analysis (Step 7). Procedures for preparing data, as well as for performing the next step, data analysis (Step 8), have been accomplished with computers for years. However, an increasing number of statistical-analysis systems for microcomputers are becoming available (cf. Neffendorf, 1983; Stemmer & Berger, 1985). Moreover, the microcomputer can make possible an intermediate step between error detection and correction, with the data then transferred to a mainframe for analysis.

Once the data have been interpreted, the researcher can write the report on a computer utilizing a word-processing program (Step 9) and can use other software programs such as *Grammatik*™ or *Sensible Grammar*™ to check the document for grammar and spelling errors. Finally, desktop presentation packages such as *Aldus Persuasion*® or *Microsoft PowerPoint*® can aid in dissemination of the study results.

## SUMMARY

The impact of computer technology on the research process cannot be overestimated. Microcomputers have touched virtually every aspect of the research process and have the potential to effect profound changes in social science research. In the next chapter we explore the research cycle by discovering how the microcomputer can help us generate problem statements. We also demonstrate how it can help us find out what others have already learned about our problem.

# 2

# Beginning the Research

## INTRODUCTION

In Chapter 1 we describe the research cycle as two overlapping "wheels" and note that the cyclical nature of the research process means that we can begin a research project almost anywhere in the cycle. As a matter of fact, many graduate students are first attracted to research as a result of their experience in gathering or analyzing someone else's data. Others may be exposed to a potential research topic by helping a principal investigator prepare results for presentation.

Each step within the cycle can be broken down further. Table 2.1, for example, illustrates the types of applications and the uses for which they might be employed at Step 1, idea processing, and Step 2, electronic abstracts and bibliographic databases.

As illustrated in Figure 2.1, our example begins at a typical starting point, the beginning of a new research project. The first thing we must do is state the general issue or problem that we intend to address. This statement will lead us through the entire process, although as we review relevant literature, we may find ourselves needing to refine it.

The first thing we need to do is generate ideas about just what problem we want to research. Sometimes that simply means writing down ideas on paper, or perhaps "brainstorming"—recording ideas as they come to mind, without critically evaluating them—in front of a blackboard with some colleagues. It is important to begin early to fashion a general idea of the question you want to address and the variables that might affect that question.

TABLE 2.1.    Research Matrix for Steps 1 and 2 of the Research Cycle

| Research Task | Application | Use |
| --- | --- | --- |
| **Step 1. State the General Issue or Problem** | | |
| Brainstorming Ideas | Idea Processing | Outlines are very useful for planning or "brainstorming." The basic notion of the idea processor is to help the user to generate ideas in a fluid way. Lower-order ideas accompany higher-order ideas, even when moved from one section of the outline to another. This flexibility can be very useful in outlining research plans. |
| **Step 2. Find Out What Others Have Learned** | | |
| Bibliographic Research | Electronic Abstracts and Bibliographic Databases | The literature review is a critical step in formulating all studies. From the literature review, the researcher can synthesize appropriate problem statements, derive supporting theoretical or conceptual models, and investigate relevant research designs. Searches of the bibliographic literature in a database located on a mainframe computer can be conducted by using the microcomputer as a terminal and saving the results in an electronic file. Alternatively, CD-ROM programs allow the user to perform comprehensive searches entirely on a microcomputer. The resultant search can then be imported directly into a personal electronic database. The personal electronic database, in turn, can be used to search relevant citations and to produce a finished bibliography. |

## IDEA PROCESSORS

An idea processor is similar to a word processor, except that it is designed to organize and reorganize thoughts and ideas quickly. There are several methods which idea processors can employ. *MORE II*™ is a visual tool that allows you to arrange ideas with text or graphics in a hierarchical order. For example, imagine that we are interested in the mathematical problem-solving skills of elementary-age school-

FIGURE 2.1.  The Beginning of the Research Cycle

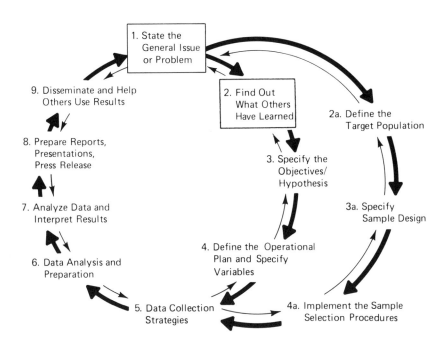

children. We could outline subtopics related to this problem as shown in Figure 2.2.

Next, suppose we wanted to continue "brainstorming" but wished to expand our ideas on the mathematics subtopic. We can provide *MORE II* commands that expand the idea, as illustrated in Figure 2.3.

Just as we expanded the mathematics section to include more ideas, we can again collapse the display to hide these ideas under the subsection so that it is balanced with the other two subtopics. The information remains intact; it is just hidden from view. Collapsing and expanding portions of the outline allow us to see and manipulate information at different levels of complexity. If we would like to change the order of the outline, we may do so, and all subordinate information will transfer with that section.

Another handy feature of idea processors such as *MORE II* is the capability to create overhead transparencies or slides that allow you to share your ideas with colleagues.* Demonstrating *MORE II* with a projection device is extremely useful for leading a group dis-

---

*We also use *MORE II* for class presentations.

cussion and planning research. When the group has completed its planning, a copy of the document can be printed for each member as he or she leaves. Figure 2.4 is an example of what an overhead transparency for our research example might look like.

FIGURE 2.2.  Beginning an Outline in *MORE II*

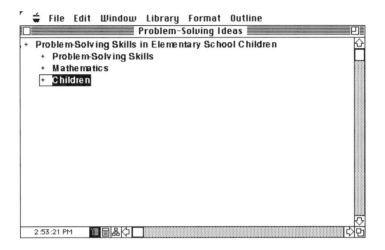

FIGURE 2.3.  Expanding an Outline in *MORE II*

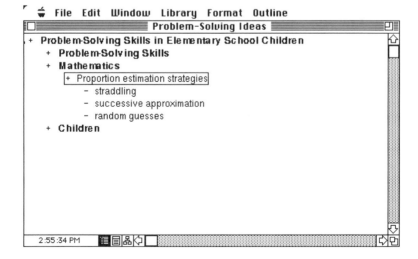

FIGURE 2.4. Bulletin Charts Created in *MORE II*

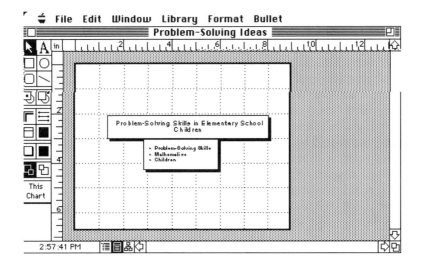

## Idea Processors

| Apple Family | Apple Macintosh | IBM PC |
|---|---|---|
| ThinkTank<br>Symantec Corp.<br>10201 Torre Ave.<br>Cupertino, CA 95015<br>(800)441-7234<br>(800)626-8847 in CA | MORE II<br>Symantec Corp.<br>10201 Torre Ave.<br>Cupertino, CA 95015<br>(800)441-7234<br>(800)626-8847 in CA | ThinkTank<br>Symantec Corp.<br>10201 Torre Ave.<br>Cupertino, CA 95015<br>(800)441-7234<br>(800)626-8847 in CA |
| Success with Writing<br>Scholastic, Inc.<br>P.O. Box 7502<br>2931 E. McCarty St.<br>Jefferson City, MO 65102<br>(800)541-5513 | Aldus Persuasion 2.0<br>Aldus Corporation<br>411 First Ave. S. Ste. 200<br>Seattle, WA 98104<br>(206)622-5500 | Lotus Agenda<br>Lotus Development Corp.<br>55 Cambridge Parkway<br>Cambridge, MA 02142<br>(617)577-8500 |
| MECC Outliner<br>MECC<br>3490 Lexington Ave. N.<br>St. Paul, MN 55126-8097<br>(612)481-3500 | Inspiration 2.0<br>Ceres Software, Inc.<br>2520 S.W. Hamilton St.<br>Portland, OR 97201<br>(503)245-9011 | Brainstormer<br>Soft Path Systems<br>c/o Chesire House<br>106 N. Adams<br>Eugene, OR 97402<br>(800)843-7243 |

## BIBLIOGRAPHIC RETRIEVAL SYSTEMS

Once we have determined what problem we are interested in pursu-
ing (so far, computers seem to be of very little help here), we continue
the research process by finding out what others know. Often the very
first place we look is to our friends and colleagues. We approach
them with questions such as, "What do you know about. . .?" or "Do
you know anyone who is studying. . .?" and so on. One way of ac-
complishing this through technology is by using *computer conferencing*—using the microcomputer as a terminal to contact colleagues
around the world to communicate, discuss, and ask questions. Features of telecommunications are discussed in Chapter 3.

As a researcher, you probably are familiar with the various
journal catalog systems, such as ERIC-RIE, Sociological Abstracts, and
Dissertation Abstracts. With the problem you have in mind, you may
be prepared to sit in front of a table of indexes for hours, printing
note cards to yourself, generating new ideas, and, of course, creating
a list of journal articles you must read for your background review.

One scholarly activity that results from this process is constructing a personal bibliographic database system. These systems
have been available on mainframe computers for almost two decades, but have been available for microcomputer systems only in
the last five years or so. Some mainframe databases contain more
than four million citations. Rapid search and retrieval by computer
is the only feasible way to explore such enormous amounts of information.

A bibliographic database works similarly to a manual filing system. Each article, book, paper, report, etc., contains its own entry.
Entries typically consist of bibliographical information (e.g., author,
year, name of article, journal title, volume, issue, page numbers); an
abstract or summary; a place for notes and observations; and cross-
reference information. Obviously, the database is only as complete
as you make it, and it takes skill to maximize the utility of the system.
An electronic database has several potential advantages over manual
systems, such as:

1. The ability to search for specific titles, authors, or key
   words by specifying the appropriate field enables you to
   search large numbers of citations in seconds.
2. Electronic databases specify a "form" for the citation information. This specification helps prompt the user to make
   more complete records, resulting in "better" bibliographic
   information.

3. Sharing information with colleagues is made easier by copying (or *exporting*—copying information in a standard computer format) the database and sending it to them.
4. Electronic databases are more portable (a floppy disk which is $\frac{1}{8}$ inch thick and $3\frac{1}{2}$ inches square can contain well over 20,000 citations; that would take a rather large file box of index cards) and more secure (back-up copies are easy to make, requiring only a few seconds, and take up very little storage space).
5. Information from electronic databases is easy to transfer from one application to the next. You need enter the citation only once.

Of course, there are some potential disadvantages as well:

1. You need access to a computer and the relevant software in order to have a working database, and you may need a little training on how to use it. While many individuals have access to computers at home, few libraries have microcomputers available for public use (although this is changing). If you are working in the library, you may have to write down the information on an index card anyway, so re-entering the citation in an electronic database can be redundant.*
2. If your work is of a sensitive nature, the feature of easy copying may be a disadvantage rather than an advantage. There are now computer "utility" packages which can encrypt information if security is a requirement.
3. Making back-up copies of electronic media requires planning and discipline. If you fail to make them, you can lose (or inadvertently destroy) valuable information and will have no other recourse than to re-enter the data.[†]

## Mainframe Bibliographic Databases

Many government, business, and academic institutions have access to a number of large mainframe information-retrieval systems

---

*Unless, of course, you happen to have a laptop or notebook computer to type the information from abstracts in the library.
[†]For most people, this happens only once. One trial learning of this concept is common.

such as BRS, DIALOG, or SDC/ORBIT. If your institution does not have a
link to these systems, you can acquire your own individual link by
subscribing to **BRS** After Dark (BRS), Knowledge Index (DIALOG), or
CompuServe (IQUEST). Each information-retrieval system contains
hundreds of databases, each of which may contain millions of citations. For example, DIALOG contains the following databases, among
others:

1. BOOK1—*Books in Print*: a comprehensive source of information on books currently in print in the United States,
   books about to be published (as far as six months in ad-
   vance), and titles declared out of print or out of stock indef-
   initely since 1979.
2. COMP3—Microcomputer Index: contains citations on the
   use of microcomputers in business, education, and the
   home. It includes magazine articles, software and hardware
   reviews, announcements of new products, and book reviews.
3. EDUC1—ERIC: complete source of educational materials
   collected by the Educational Resources Information Center
   (ERIC) of the National Institute of Education (NIE), U.S. Department of Education. It includes virtually all types of
   print materials, published and unpublished, that deal with
   education.
4. PSYC1—PsycInfo: covers the world's literature in psychology and related behavioral and social sciences, such as psy-
   chiatry, sociology, anthropology, education, pharmacology,
   and linguistics.
5. REFR5—Dissertation Abstracts Online: comprehensive listing of virtually every American dissertation accepted at an
   accredited institution since 1861, plus citations for thousands of Canadian dissertations and an increasing number
   of papers accepted abroad. Dissertations for professional
   and honorary degrees are not included. All subject areas are
   listed.
6. SOCS1—Sociological Abstracts: covers the world's literature in sociology and related disciplines in the social and behavioral sciences. Over 1600 journals and other serial
   publications are scanned each year to provide coverage of
   orginal research, reviews, discussions, monographic publications, panel discussions, and case studies. Conference papers and dissertations also are indexed.

In contrast to the general databases listed above, most main-frame bibliographic retrieval services contain information sources which address very specific topics. For example, there are specialized databases for drug abuse and AIDS, among others. There are even specialized databases devoted solely to microcomputers and microcomputer products.

Borg and Gall (1989) have an excellent introduction to searching a bibliographic database. They recommend seven steps in conducting a search of an electronic database. Notice that these steps are very similar to the flow of information in the research cycle.

1. *Define the research problem.* You need to articulate a short but precise statement of the research problem. For our example, our statement of the research problem could be: "What problem-solving strategies do children use when they estimate mathematical ratios?" Keep in mind that in order to formulate a statement of the problem, you must have a basic familiarity with the topic. The term "cognitive strategies" could be discussed just as easily in the research as "problem-solving." Only knowledge of the literature will help you make a choice of one term over another. Using the wrong terminology can lead to less-than-fruitful results.

2. *State the specific purpose of your search.* Do you want a broad review of all possibly relevant literature, or do you want to narrow down your search for a specific purpose (e.g., to locate a measurement instrument.) Are you interested in a specific subgroup? (In our example, we are interested in children.) Are you looking for references to a certain author? Within a limited period of time (e.g., after 1985)?

3. *Select the database.* As mentioned before, there are hundreds of databases from which to choose. A description of the database can be obtained from documentation provided by the information-retrieval company. Note that your search may be constrained by limitations on (a) the previously reported research in the area, (b) the time available on the system, and (c) the money allocated for the search. For purposes of our demonstration, we chose the ERIC database, but could have followed up with a search of the PsycInfo and SOCIAL SCISEARCH databases.

4. *Select the descriptors.* Key words in the literature usually are common to the relevant database. The operative word

here, however, is "usually." Depending on the purpose of your search, you may have to consult a thesaurus to investigate related, expanded, or restricted phrases. For our example—the problem-solving strategies of children in estimating mathematical ratios—we consulted the *Thesaurus of ERIC Descriptors* to see which terms would be most appropriate. For example, consider the term "mathematical." For our target age group, the term "arithmetic" sometimes is used instead of "mathematics." However, after a quick investigation of the *Thesaurus*, we decided that "mathematics" would give us more relevant citations.

5. *Plan the computer search.* Computers use Boolean logic in conducting bibliographic searches. The Venn diagram shown in Figure 2.5 illustrates how a Boolean search might be operationalized. The overlap in the center of the diagram represents the intersection of three terms germane to the literature in which we are interested—"Problem Solving" *and* "Mathematics" *and* "Children." Notice our use of the connector *"and."* If we had wanted to expand the scope of our search, we could have used "Problem Solving" *or* "Cognitive Strategies" *and* "Mathematics"; the use of the *"or"* connector would expand our first term. Had we left out the restriction "Children," our search would have resulted in citations involving children, adolescents, and adults.

FIGURE 2.5.  Intersection of Three Bodies of Literature for the Problem-Solving Example

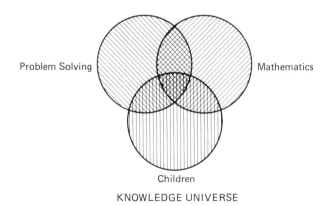

KNOWLEDGE UNIVERSE

6. *Conduct the search.* Figure 2.6 shows a log of the interactive search of the DIALOG database ERIC.* Included in the output is one abstract from the 22 which the search identified.

   This session went very quickly (.163 hours, or 9.78 minutes) and did not cost very much (approximately $8.80). Most searches cost in the neighborhood of $20–$30; discounts are offered for searches run during off-peak hours (usually at night or during weekends, when crazed researchers are working anyway).

   The DIALOG information-retrieval system offers eight different output formats, including citation only, citation and abstract, and full article text.[†]

7. *Review the printout.* Information retrieval is a skill. Even standard combinations of key words may sometimes result in a strange selection of articles. In your review of the printout, you may find that the types of articles you thought you were going to obtain never materialized. As a result, you may need to reconsider your database or key word descriptors, or even reformulate your problem statement. Think of your search efforts as an iterative process, much like an artist chipping away at stone—the more times you do it, the more productive the result.

In order to save money in this process, you may wish to list only 10–20 citations for your initial review. If you happen to hit paydirt and obtain a reasonable number of relevant citations, you can list the remaining ones in a subsequent run. Special training on bibliographic retrieval is offered by DIALOG and other vendors.

## Microcomputerized Bibliographic Databases

We have characterized the types of microcomputerized bibliographic database systems as professional and personal. Typically, the professional microcomputerized bibliographic database is a replication of its mainframe counterpart, but has been configured spe-

*This sometimes is referred to as a "buffered conversation," meaning that the information on the screen is being stored in the computer's memory. The software used in this process may permit the information to be stored on disk as well.

[†]Many combinations are possible, but, as you might suspect, obtaining the full text of an article can be an expensive option.

## FIGURE 2.6. Electronic Record of a Search Conducted with Dialog Information Services, Inc.

```
TERMINAL=d1
@C 415 48D
415 48D    CONNECTED
DIALOG INFORMATION SERVICES
PLEASE LOGON:
********
ENTER PASSWORD:
********
Welcome to DIALOG
Dialog version 2, level 12.4.6 A

Last logoff 11mar90 09:52:13
Logon file001 11mar90 16:38:32

File 1:ERIC - 66-90/FEB

    Set Items Description
    --- ----- ---------
?ss problem solving and mathematics/maj and children/de
    S1 11409 PROBLEM SOLVING
    S2 17384 MATHEMATICS/MAJ
    S3 27548 CHILDREN/DE (AGED BIRTH THROUGH APPROXIMATELY 12 YEARS)
    S4 22 PROBLEM SOLVING AND MATHEMATICS/MAJ AND CHILDREN/DE
?t 4/5/all
4/5/1
EJ340412 PS514464
    Relationship of Elementary School Children's Private Speech to Behavioral
Accompaniment to Task, Attention, and Task Performance.
    Berk, Laura E.
    Developmental Psychology, v22 n5 p671-80 Sep 1986
    Available from: UMI
    Language: English
    Document Type: JOURNAL ARTICLE (080); RESEARCH REPORT (143)
    Journal Announcement: CIJDEC86
    Target Audience: Researchers
    Observes 75 first- and third-grade children in their classroom mathematics seatwork to
test assumptions drawn from Vygotsky's theory about the development of private speech
and its relationship to task performance, attention, and motor behaviors accompanying
task orientation. (HOD)
    Descriptors: *Attention Control; Children; *Cognitive Development; Developmental
Stages; Elementary School Students; Epistemology; *Intellectual Development; *Mathemat-
ics Achievement; *Problem Solving; Psycholinguistics; *Verbal Development
    Identifiers: *Private Speech; Vygotsky (Lev S)
......21 additional citations were listed here......
?logoff
    11mar90 16:48:17 User002145
    $4.89 0.163 Hrs File1
    $2.20 22 Types in Format 5
    $2.20 22 Types
    $1.79 Telenet
    $8.88 Estimated cost this file
    $8.88 Estimated total session cost 0.163 Hrs.
Logoff: level 12.4.6 A 16:48:17
```

cifically for the microcomputer. For example, versions of the ERIC and PsycInfo databases can be purchased on CD-ROM. The expense of CD-ROM players, software, and the subscription usually means that they are purchased by large institutions, such as libraries or academic departments. To search the information that might be in the ERIC system, one need only go to the microcomputer and access the CD-ROM by means of a search strategy similar to that of the mainframe system. ERIC CD-ROM is now available for **IBM-PC/XT/AT** computers and compatibles.

The personal microcomputerized database enables the user to create his or her own citation index system, not only for abstracts and notekeeping, but to compile bibliographies as well. Moreover, sophisticated personal databases will take input directly from the mainframe database, so the user need never again type a single abstract.

Examples of creating a database, transferring information from a mainframe database to a personal database, searching for information, and creating a bibliography are given in the annotated screens illustrated in Figures 2.7 through 2.9. Our example is taken from *Pro-Cite®* (with *Biblio-Link®*) from Personal Bibliographic Software, Inc.,

FIGURE 2.7. Program Start-up Screen for *Pro-Cite*

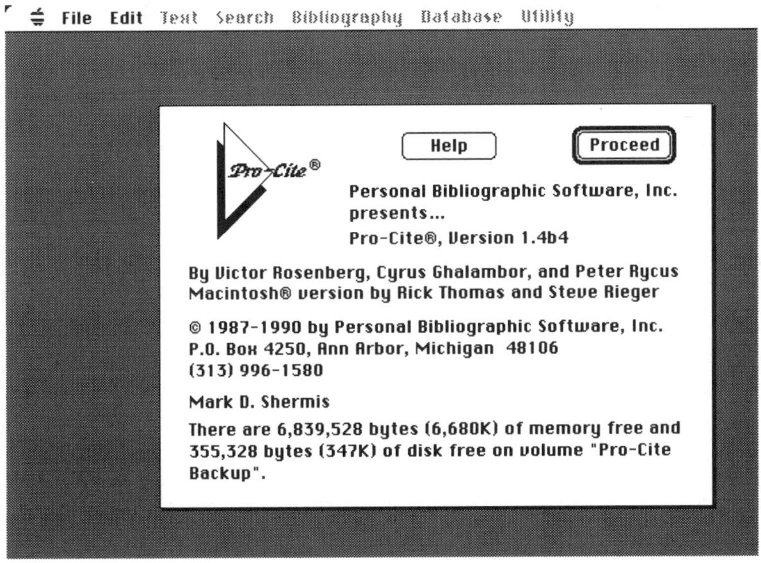

FIGURE 2.8.  Creating a New Database in *Pro-Cite*

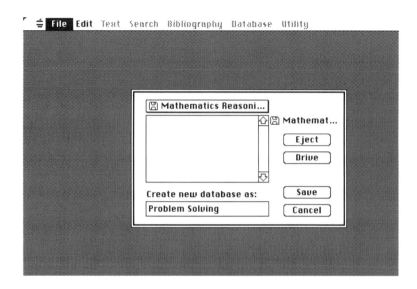

FIGURE 2.9.  Choosing a Citation Form in *Pro-Cite*

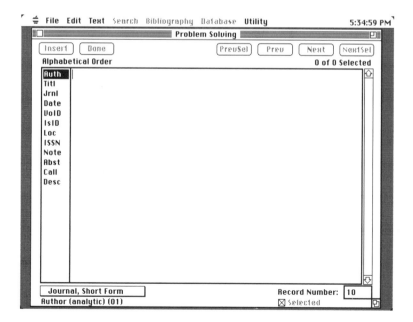

for the Apple Macintosh. A parallel version of the software is available for MS-DOS machines.

The first thing you'll be asked to do is to open a new database for use in *Pro-Cite*. In our example, we call the new database "Problem Solving." We store the file on our "Mathematics Research" disk.

Next, we need to choose a format into which the bibliographic information can be placed. *Pro-Cite*, developed by library information specialists, has more than 20 formats for entry and retrieval of bibliographical information. Common formats include those for books, journals, reports, conference proceedings, newspapers, dissertations, computer programs, and audiovisual material, among others. The advantage of a system like this is that the *Pro-Cite* programmers have built in artificial intelligence routines for bibliographic retrieval. The program "knows" what questions (e.g., fields of information) to ask, according to the type of material sought. Let's begin by selecting a common citation form: Journal, Short Form.*

In our example, the mainframe search of the topic "Problem Solving" resulted in 22 citations. Eight citations related to articles, ten to conference proceedings, one to a book, and three to reports. *Biblio-Link* is a series of software programs that convert the results of a mainframe computer search and enter the information directly into *Pro-Cite*. Not having to re-enter each citation into our personal database increases efficiency and accuracy considerably.

There are different versions of *Biblio-Link* which correspond to the type of service that you would use to "download" information (i.e., transfer it from the mainframe to your personal computer). For example, we conducted our search on DIALOG and therefore would use the DIALOG version of *Biblio-Link*. Other services supported include BRS, DIALOG2, RLIN, OCLC, and MEDLARS.

DIALOG offers several output formats. For example, in our run we asked DIALOG to list both citation information and abstracts (Format 5). *Biblio-Link* can detect the DIALOG format automatically, but needs to know what format to use to process the citation. We indicated to *Biblio-Link* that we are interested in processing Form D: Journal, Short Form. Figure 2.10 shows how this software configuration is accomplished.

Because *Biblio-Link* processes one bibliographic form at a time, it may be necessary for you to divide your log file (in our example, it was called "Archived Screens")† into subfiles. To break up the file,

---

*Journal, Long Form is another option.
†The conversation buffer file was created by *Red Ryder*™ 10.3, a popular telecommunications package. See the section on telecommunications for additional information on this process.

FIGURE 2.10. Configuring a Citation Type in *Biblio-Link*

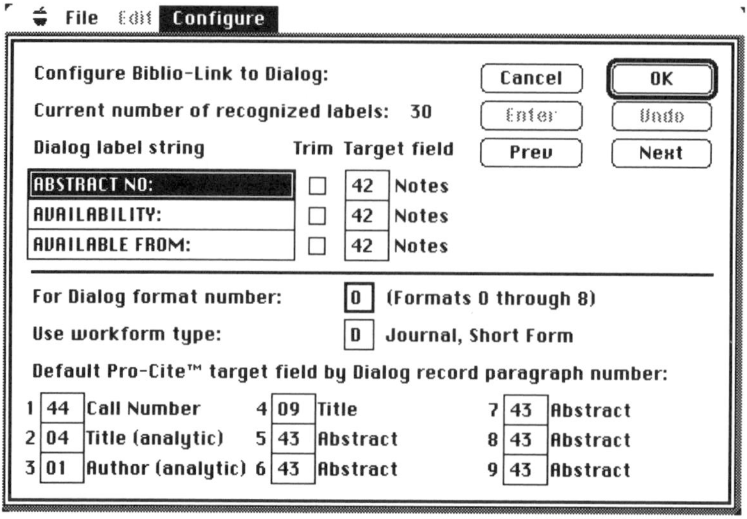

```
 ⊜  File  Edit  Configure                                                  

  Configure Biblio-Link to Dialog:              [ Cancel ]   ▐  OK  ▌
  Current number of recognized labels:   30     [ Enter  ]   [ Undo ]
  Dialog label string         Trim Target field [  Prev  ]   [ Next ]

  ▐ABSTRACT NO:           ▌     □   42  Notes
   AVAILABILITY:                □   42  Notes
   AVAILABLE FROM:              □   42  Notes

  For Dialog format number:        [0]  (Formats 0 through 8)
  Use workform type:               [D]  Journal, Short Form
  Default Pro-Cite™ target field by Dialog record paragraph number:
  1│44│Call Number      4│09│Title       7│43│Abstract
  2│04│Title (analytic) 5│43│Abstract    8│43│Abstract
  3│01│Author (analytic)6│43│Abstract    9│43│Abstract
```

you can use a simple file editor (e.g., *Edit*, a text file editor distributed by Apple Computer, Inc.) or any word processor that handles ASCII text files.* As shown in Figure 2.11, we broke up the file into subfiles named "Dialog.art" (articles), "Dialog.paper" (conference papers), "Dialog.book" (books), and "Dialog.rep" (reports). In our example, we chose the file "Dialog.art" to read into the database first.

Figure 2.12 shows that *Biblio-Link* successfully processed eight of the citations/abstracts that were stored in the file "Dialog.art."

Figure 2.13 shows the bibliographic entry for one of the articles. Keep in mind that not one bit of information had to be typed directly into the database.

Subsequent processing to the other subfiles (e.g., papers, books, reports) produced a database of 22 entries on the topic "Problem Solving." This, of course, was the result of only one search of the ERIC database; searches of other databases probably would produce additional citations. As mentioned previously, the electronic database has a number of potential uses. In Figure 2.14 we illustrate a search being conducted on an author key word, although other fields also could have been used.

---

*ASCII stands for American Standard Codes II. An ASCII file is also called a "text file" and usually is compatible with most computers. It contains only information about numbers and letters without unusual commands or characters.

FIGURE 2.11. Processing the File "Dialog.art" in *Biblio-Link*

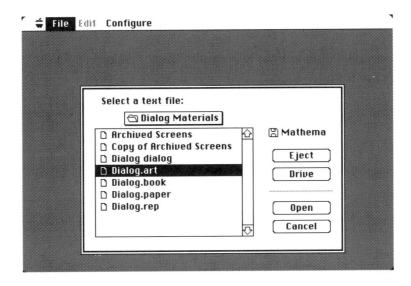

FIGURE 2.12. File "Dialog.art" Successfully Processed in
*Biblio-Link*

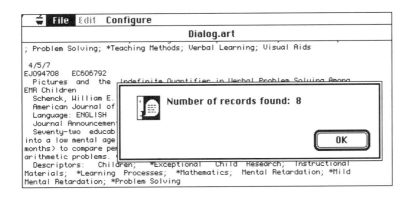

Finally, one of the handy features of *Pro-Cite* is its ability to create a bibliography of selected database entries. *Pro-Cite* allows you to select among many journal formats, including American National Standards Insitute (ANSI), Modern Library Association (MLA), Science, and American Psychological Association (APA).

Figure 2.15 is a partial bibliography from our search of "Problem Solving," listed in APA format. The bibliography usually can be

FIGURE 2.13. Displaying a Sample Entry in the ''Problem Solving'' *Pro-Cite* Database

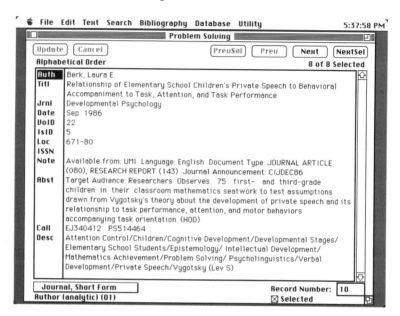

appended to a file containing the research report (e.g., article) by a standard word-processing package. Part of the effort required to create the electronic database is offset, therefore, by a decrease in the typing required to generate a bibliographic listing. This is especially true if your research tends to use the same citations from one study to the next.

The researcher who does not wish to pay the extra cost of bibliographic software can use a standard database-management program or even a word processor. The advantage in using a database-management or word-processing program is that they can be used for other activities in the research cycle. Many word processors can transfer information from the database-management software automatically into a word-processing document.

The most significant disadvantage of a standard database-management software or word-processing package becomes apparent once you have used a bibliographic software system. The professional systems already have done the work of designing the fields and the report formats. A standard database-management system usually is capable of formatting the citations properly, but the set-up

## FIGURE 2.14. Specifying an Author Search in *Pro-Cite*

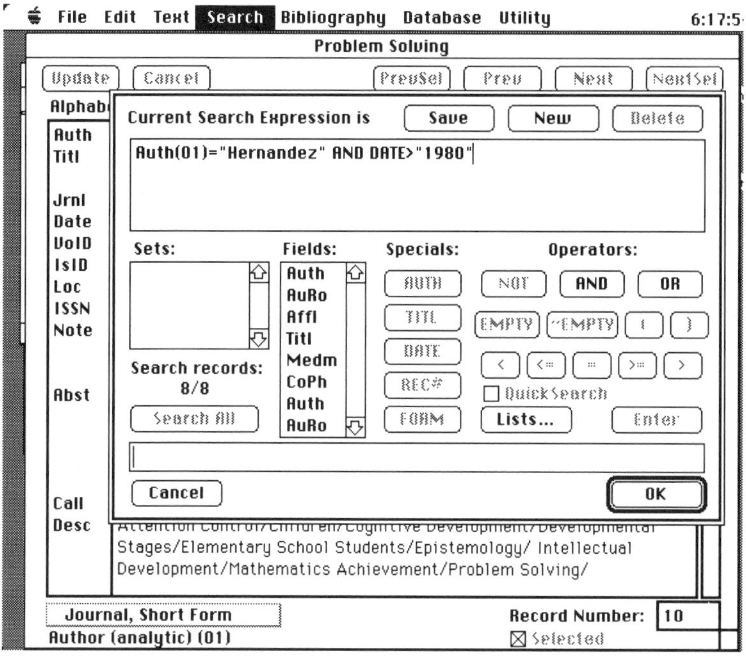

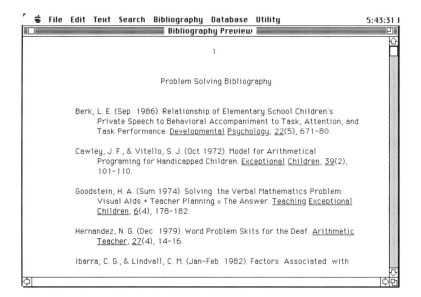

**FIGURE 2.15.** Listing a Bibliography in APA Format in *Pro-Cite*

## Electronic Abstracts/Bibliographic Databases

| Apple Family | Apple Macintosh | IBM PC |
|---|---|---|
| Bookends Extended<br>Sensible Software, Inc.<br>335 E. Big Beaver, Ste. 207<br>Troy, MI 48083<br>(313)528-1950 | Pro-Cite<br>Personal Bibliographic<br>Software, Inc.<br>P.O. Box 4250<br>Ann Arbor, MI 48106<br>(313)996-1580 | Pro-Cite<br>Personal Bibliographic<br>Software, Inc.<br>P.O. Box 4250<br>Ann Arbor, MI 48106<br>(313)996-1580 |
| Librarian<br>Dynacomp, Inc.<br>178 Phillips Rd.<br>Webster, NY 14580<br>(716)265-4040 | EndNote<br>Niles & Associates<br>2200 Powell St., Ste. 765<br>Emeryville, CA 94608<br>(415)655-6666 | Publish or Perish<br>Park Row Software<br>4640 Jewell St. #232<br>San Diego, CA 92109<br>(619)581-6778 |
| Research Manager<br>Sather Ruth and Associates<br>2120 Moonlight Bay Dr.<br>Altoona, WI 54720<br>(715)835-5020 | Bookends Mac<br>Sensible Software, Inc.<br>335 E. Big Beaver, Ste. 207<br>Troy, MI 48083<br>(313)528-1950 | Notebook II Plus<br>Oberon Resources<br>147 East Oakland Ave.<br>Columbus OH 43201<br>(614)294-7762 |
| | RefMaker<br>Cat's Cradle Software<br>P.O. Box 684<br>Ann Arbor, MI 48106<br>(313)665-6152 | PC-Bibliography<br>Elcomp Publishing, Inc.<br>4650 Arrow Hwy., Unit A3<br>Montclair, CA 91763<br>(714)626-4070 |

## Bibliographic Links

| Apple Family | Apple Macintosh | IBM PC |
|---|---|---|
| | Biblio-Link & Pro-Search<br>Personal Bibliographic<br>Software, Inc.<br>P.O. Box 4250<br>Ann Arbor, MI 48106<br>(313)996-1580 | Biblio-Link & Pro-Search<br>Personal Bibliographic<br>Software, Inc.<br>P.O. Box 4250<br>Ann Arbor, MI 48106<br>(313)996-1580 |
| | EndLink<br>Niles & Associates<br>2200 Powell St., Ste. 765<br>Emeryville, CA 94608<br>(415)655-6666 | Q-Base<br>Online Research Systems,<br>Inc.<br>2901 Broadway, Ste. 154<br>New York, NY 10025<br>(212)408-3311 |

time may be considerable, and with database-management or word-processing packages, you must do it on your own. Databases are discussed more fully in Chapter 6.

## SUMMARY

Outlines can be very useful for planning programs of study. An idea processor can help the user generate and communicate ideas in a fluid way. By manipulating the outline, ideas can be restructured, placed in a unique context, or simply explored in a different way, without a major commitment to word-processing efforts. This flexibility can be very useful in "brainstorming."

The literature review is a critical step in structuring the research study. From the literature review, the researcher can synthesize appropriate problem statements, derive supporting theoretical or conceptual models, and investigate relevant research designs. Searches of the bibliographic literature in a database located on a mainframe computer can be conducted by using the microcomputer as a terminal and saving the results in an electronic file. Alternatively, CD-ROM programs allow the user to perform comprehensive searches entirely on a microcomputer. The resultant search then can be imported directly into a personal electronic database. The personal electronic database, in turn, can be used to identify relevant citations and to produce a finished bibliography.

In the next chapter we continue planning our research study by focusing on the administrative steps that need to be taken in order to get the job done. Just as it does in the business world, the microcomputer will help a great deal.

# 3

# Planning the Research: Administrative

## INTRODUCTION

There are many administrative tasks that must be anticipated before the research begins. A good piece of research usually is the result of good planning. The activities in this chapter, summarized in Table 3.1, illustrate how to plan the research, monitor progress, and administer the program. We list these activities under Step 3 because they interact with the operational planning steps listed in the next chapter. In addition, the specification of the ultimate study objectives is dependent in part on the researcher's ability to collect data. Administrative planning can help shape this process.

The experienced researcher knows that not everything will go according to plan. If the test publisher can't get the instrument shipped to you on time, then your plans have to change. If the departmental subject pool is overbooked, then someone may have to put off an experiment. Adequate funding for good research is always necessary; someone has to pay the bills. What if the funding agency mandates a 10% across-the-board cut in everyone's budget?

Many researchers find planning and managing the research study the most tedious part of the research cycle. A number of software packages can make this part of the research process more manageable and efficient, although still not much fun. The more the process is automated, the more time the researcher can devote to the fun part—conducting the study, interpreting results, and writing the report.

Figure 3.1 shows where we are in the cycle of planning the re-

TABLE 3.1.   Research Matrix for Step 3 of the Research Cycle

| Research Task | Application | Use |
|---|---|---|
| **Step 3. Specify the Objectives/Hypotheses** | | |
| Grant Monitoring | Telecommunications Software | We access mainframes by using the microcomputer as an intelligent terminal. We can look through a variety of on-line mainframe databases of public and private grants. When a grant of interest is found, we can download the information onto the disk for word processing and electronic mail distribution. |
| Budgeting | Spreadsheets | Resource monitoring is an important part of the research process and must be done carefully. Spreadsheet software is available to help the researcher quickly and easily create budgets, which will help assess the feasibility of a given project. |
| Project Monitoring | Project Management Software | Anticipating problems is perhaps the most critical task of any principal investigator. Not everything goes according to the researcher's "Plan A." Project monitoring will help the investigator foresee when "Plan B" might be required and help outline the steps necessary to tackle problems that occasionally arise. |
| Creating Draft Proposals, Written Plans | Word Processing | Word processing is the most basic and fundamental tool of the researcher. Drafts are written and circulated to the staff and changes easily made. File revising and archiving are very simple and require little physical storage space. In addition, word-processing and desktop-publishing software can be used to produce a very polished grant proposal. Because previous proposals are maintained on file, standard explanations and descriptions of personnel and facilities can be used repeatedly without having to retype them. Proposals can be put together much more quickly and efficiently because they require less effort and time. |

FIGURE 3.1.  Planning the Research

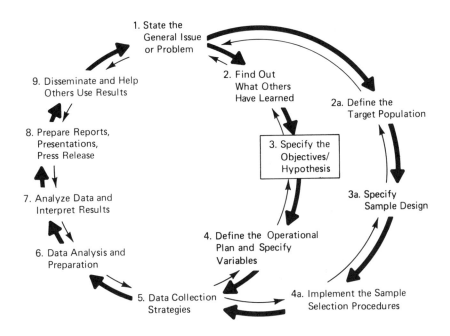

search study. Of course, research can be done independently of a funded program, but for our purposes we start this chapter with an examination of how grants can be monitored electronically. We then use spreadsheet software to create a prototypical research budget, then follow up with software designed to help plan and manage a research program. Finally, we examine word-processing software that can be especially useful in responding to RFPs (Requests For Proposals).

## GRANT MONITORING WITH TELECOMMUNICATIONS SOFTWARE

A common frustration of grantsmanship is that often by the time one receives an RFP, the grant deadline is about to pass. Typically, one receives notification of impending RFPs through publications such as the *Federal Register, Commerce Business Daily,* the *Chronicle of Higher Education,* or some other printed medium. These time-honored dissemination mechanisms work well, but are rather expensive in both time and money for the typical researcher. For example, a subscription to *Commerce Business Daily* costs several hundred dollars per year. Even where there is a central library for journals and papers, administrative delays may prevent publications from getting into researchers' hands in time to prepare an adequate response. One may be on the mailing list for RFP notices within a government bureau or department, but these units do not tend to coordinate grant information. Even though a researcher may be in touch with one department or bureau, he or she may not be aware of what another department currently is supporting.

A number of professional organizations recently have sought to improve the dissemination of funding information. For example, the American Psychological Association (APA) posts the *Science Directorate Funding Bulletin*, which is updated through computer links to a researcher's institutional mainframe computer account via BITNET (Because It's Time Network). BITNET is an international telecommunications network that allows academic researchers to send messages/data for little or no direct cost. The network essentially is underwritten by the consortium of schools that subscribe to EDUCOM.* Messages/data are restricted to approximately 25 kilobytes of information (25,000 characters), must be generated from a computer account on a mainframe at a host institution, and should have a legitimate research purpose. The 25-kilobyte restriction is sometimes constraining, but usually is sufficient to accommodate modest data sets, articles, or book chapters. We used BITNET to communicate with each other while writing this book.[†]

## Telecommunications

What is telecommunications? Telecommunications networks use either local voice-telephone lines or "hard-wired" lines (dedicated phone lines used to transmit pictures, audio, or computer data) to connect to broader networks of mainframes or minicomputers. If voice-phone lines are used, a modem (*modulator-dem*odulator) translates electronic digital signals into sound signals that are translated back into digital signals by the host computer. Phone networks specifically established to transmit electronically encoded data form the heart of telecommunications. Examples of such networks include AUTONET, TELENET, and TYMNET.

---

*EDUCOM's address is P.O. Box 364, Princeton, NJ 08540. Phone: (609)520-3350
[†]BITNET has begun to add on "gateways" to other networks. For example, it is now possible to send a message to an individual on CompuServe (a commercial telecommunications network) from a BITNET address.

Communication over networks uses various protocols and takes place at various speeds. Protocols are rules governing the way computer modems transmit to one another. The most common form of communication over a network uses an asynchronous protocol. *Asynchronous* communication is characterized by character-by-character transmission and is designed for interactive communication at human typing speeds. It is the most common form of communications protocol because of its ease of transmission by standard telephone lines. Where networks involve the use of telephone systems (and many do), this can be an important consideration. *Synchronous* communication, by contrast, means high-speed, block-by-block transmission. It is designed for both interactive and batch processing and generally is more expensive than asynchronous service. Figures 3.2 and 3.3 show the introductory and help screens for *ProComm*™, a popular telecommunications package for MS-DOS-based machines. *ProComm* is distributed as "shareware," meaning that you can copy the program, try it out for awhile, and send the developer a stipulated amount of money if you decide you want to continue using the program,. The payment of fees usually entitles you to upgrades of the program when they are released. The "shareware" concept was implemented to keep the cost of software to a minimum. It relies solely on the "honor system" to make it work.

FIGURE 3.2. The Initialization Screen for *ProComm* (MS-DOS)

Version 2.4.2
(C) 1985, 1986 Datastorm Technologies, Inc. (Formerly PIL Software Systems)

This is a user supported product. It is not public domain, and it is not free software. You are granted a limited license to use this product on a trial basis. If you wish to continue using the product after the trial period you must register by sending: (a) $25 for registration only (no disk), (b) $35 for registration plus the latest version on disk, or (c) $50 for registration, disk and printed, bound manual to the address below. Missouri residents please add 4.3% sales tax.

ProComm support BBS: (314) 449-9401  24 hours per day, 7 days per week.

Thank you for your support!

=== Datastorm Technologies, Inc.  PO Box 1471  Columbia, MO 65205 ===

FIGURE 3.3.  The Help Screen for ProComm

```
                        P r o C o m m   H e l p




Dialing Directory . Alt-D  Program Info ...... Alt-I  Send files ...... PgUp
Automatic Redial... Alt-R  Setup Screen ...... Alt-S  Receive files ... PgDn
Keyboard Macros ... Alt-M  Kermit Server Cmd . Alt-K  Directory ...... Alt-F
Line Settings ..... Alt-P  Change Directory .. Alt-B  View a File .... Alt-V
Translate Table ... Alt-W  Clear Screen ...... Alt-C  Screen Dump .... Alt-G
Editor ............ Alt-A  Toggle Duplex ..... Alt-E  Log Toggle .... Alt-F1
Exit .............. Alt-X  Hang Up Phone ..... Alt-H  Log Hold ...... Alt-F2
Host Mode ......... Alt-Q  Elapsed Time ...... Alt-T
Chat Mode ......... Alt-O  Print On/Off ...... Alt-L
DOS Gateway ...... Alt-F4  Set Colors ........ Alt-Z
Command Files .... Alt-F5  Auto Answer ....... Alt-Y
Redisplay ........ Alt-F6  Toggle CR-CR/LF .. Alt-F3
                           Break Key ........ Alt-F7
```

The speed at which data are transmitted is referred to as baud rate. Common rates for asynchronous communications are at 300, 1200, 2400, and 9600 baud. These often are referred to as 30, 120, 240, and 960 characters-per-second (CPS) transfer rates, although there are technical differences between baud rate and CPS transfer rate. Keep in mind that a good typist can type about 100 words per minute, or about 6.5 CPS.

Typically, synchronous communication is geared toward much faster rates of transfer, around 4800–9600 baud, although synchronous communications for remote batch processing can be much slower. Synchronous communications are faster because they often support such features as full-screen editing, which requires quick interaction between the terminal and computer.* For the two computers to communicate, the protocol settings on each machine must match. Figure 3.4 shows a modem (asynchronous) connection to the

---

*With the release of high-speed (9600 baud) asynchronous modems, the differences between asynchronous and synchronous communications have become blurred as to the criterion of transmission speed.

FIGURE 3.4. *ProComm* in Action

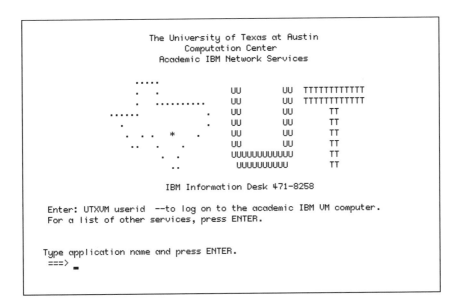

academic mainframe computer at The University of Texas at Austin using *ProComm*.

In addition to a taxonomy of protocols and speeds, communications also are characterized by the mode in which data are sent. In full-duplex mode, you and the computer can communicate simultaneously. For example, you might be typing a series of commands while the computer is printing the results of previous commands. Half-duplex mode restricts communications to one-way bursts. Either the computer or the user can communicate at any point in time, but not both. These modes can affect the way in which you communicate with your computer. Of course, half-duplex communication is much easier to effect than full-duplex because devices that handle only one-way communications are simpler than those that handle two-way communications. Moreover, extending the logic of the previous paragraphs, it is easy to see that full-duplex, synchronous communications are more complex than full-duplex, asynchronous communications. This sounds complicated, but most host computer systems have documentation or technical support staff to tell the user about correct settings. Almost all telecommunications software allows you to change settings to match the host.

## Telecommunications Software

| Apple Family | Apple Macintosh | IBM PC |
|---|---|---|
| ASCII Express-The Professional United Software Industries 8399 Topanga Blvd. Suite 200 Canoga Park, CA 91304 (818)887-5800 | White Knight The FreeSoft Co. 150 Hickory Dr. Beaver Falls, PA 15010 (412)846-2700 | ProComm (shareware) ProComm Plus (commercial) Datastorm Technologies, Inc. 1621 Towne Dr., Suite G P.O. Box 1471 Columbia, MO 65205 (314)474-8461 |
| Proterm Checkmate Technology, Inc. 509 S. Rockford Dr. Tempe, AZ 85281-3021 (602)966-5802 | MicroPhone II Software Ventures Corp. 2907 Claremont Ave. Suite 220 Berkeley, CA 94705 (415)644-3232 | PC-Talk 4 Headlands Corp. P.O. Box 8 Tiburon, CA 94920 (415)435-0770 |
| SmartCom II Hayes Microcomputer Products 705 Westech Norcross, GA 30092 (404)449-8791 | SmartCom II Hayes Microcomputer Products 705 Westech Norcross, GA 30092 (404)449-8791 | SmartCom II for the PC Hayes Microcomputer Products 705 Westech Norcross, GA 30092 (404)449-8791 |
| Softerm II Softronics, Inc. 7899 Lexington Dr. Suite 210 Colorado Springs, CO 80920 (719)593-9540 | VersaTerm-Pro Synergy Software 2457 Perkiomen Ave. Reading, PA 19606 (215)779-0522 | Softerm PC Softronics, Inc. 7899 Lexington Dr. Suite 210 Colorado Springs, CO 80920 (719)593-9540 |
| Flex-I-Term Sourceview Software Intl. P.O. Box 578 Concord, CA 94522-0578 (415)686-8439 | MacKnowledge Prometheus Products, Inc. 4545 Cushing Parkway Fremont, CA 94538 (800)477-3473 | ASCII Pro United Software Industries 8399 Topanga Blvd. Suite 200 Canoga Park, CA 91304 (818)887-5800 |

Let's return to our example from the APA's *Science Directorate Funding Bulletin* and illustrate how it works. Upon registering with the Science Directorate's Office (APASDSSW@GWUVM),* the APA member receives periodic bulletins with brief descriptions of current

---

*BITNET addresses are divided into two parts: an account (e.g., APASDSSW) and a node (e.g., GWUVM). The account name APASDSSW stands for American Psychological Association, Science Directorate Subscription, Suzanne

funding opportunities. Figures 3.5 and 3.6 show a typical funding bulletin.

Once the researcher has chosen a topic of interest, he or she sends a message to the Science Directorate's file server to obtain details about funding. Figure 3.7 shows an RFP notice disseminated by the March of Dimes for interdisciplinary social science research.

If you decide that the funding source is an appropriate match for your research ideas, you can contact the sponsor by mail, phone, or, in many cases, a computer network such as BITNET. Telecommunications can be a very efficient way to find out if there are matches between funded research and your own research topics.

## Spreadsheets

Planning a budget for your research study also will help you determine whether your topic is "researchable." That is, you may infer from your financial planning that the cost of exploring the topic is prohibitive, given the current state of research development in the field. While we're not advocating the pursuit of a study based solely on fiscal concerns, a well-done budget may show you that other, related topics might be more feasible.

A spreadsheet is a tool that facilitates various administrative and planning processes needed for research. You might think of a spreadsheet as the electronic equivalent of a large ledger with rows and columns, only far more dynamic. Rows are assigned numbers, columns are assigned letters, and at the intersection of each row and column is a cell. Data consist of numbers, formulas, or letters (which may be considered *labels*). A numeric *value*, or a *formula* for calculating the value to be placed in that cell, is a function of values entered or calculated elsewhere in the spreadsheet. Values within a cell can be displayed in several formats—dollars and cents, scientific notation, percentages, dates, and time, among others.

Formulas can be very simple, such as for adding a row or column of numbers, or they can be very complex, referring to a range of locations, or requiring considerable arithmetic, or selecting a value according to some criterion. Some examples of formulas are given in Table 3.2.

Wanderson. Suzanne is the administrator of the Funding Bulletin. GUWVM is a VM account (a type of IBM operating system) at George Washington University. Mark's BITNET address is EPFG745@UTXVM; Carl is available at USERK3HL@UMICHUM; Ernie is happy to chat with you at GEAND@UMASS.

FIGURE 3.5.  The American Psychological Association Science
Directorate Funding Bulletin


Sender:          APA Research Psychology Network <APASD-L@VTVM2>
From:            Suzanne Wandersman <APASDSSW@GWUVM>
Subject:         Current Issue of Funding Bulletin
To:              Mark Shermis <EPFG745@UTXVM>


AMERICAN PSYCHOLOGICAL ASSOCIATION SCIENCE DIRECTORATE
FUNDING BULLETIN
- - - - - - - - - - - - - - - - - - - - - - - - - - - - - - - - - - - - - - - - - - - - - - - - - - - - - - - - - - -
Volume 1, No. 8                                             July 11, 1989
- - - - - - - - - - - - - - - - - - - - - - - - - - - - - - - - - - - - - - - - - - - - - - - - - - - - - - - - - -
*************************************************************************************
*   The APA Science Directorate Funding Bulletin is designed to alert you to research and
*   training funding sources for pscyhology. Each file in the index below contains
*   summaries of recently published requests for applications (RFAs), requests for
*   proposals (RFPs), or similar documents. The index is updated regularly and distributed
*   each time new announcements are added. You may subscribe to the Bulletin by issuing
*   a SUBscribe command to APASD-L AT VTVM2 or by sending a message to
*   APASDSSW@GWUVM.
*
*   FOR MORE INFORMATION ABOUT ANY FUNDING ANNOUNCEMENT BELOW, CONTACT
*   THE INDIVIDUAL(S) IDENTIFIED IN THE FILE. BEFORE SUBMITTING AN APPLICATION FOR
*   ANY RFA OR RFP LISTED BELOW, BE SURE TO GET IN TOUCH WITH THE CONTACT
*   PERSON.
*************************************************************************************
*************************************************************************************
HOW TO REQUEST FILES
*   Most BITNET users can request files from LISTSERV at node VTVM2. If you entered the
*   command correctly and all the links between nodes are functional, your request will be
*   acknowledged and the file you requested should arrive in your reader file. The
*   command for requesting files is as follows:
*
*   Type the following command, at the "ready prompt," if you are using a CMS system:
*
*       TELL LISTSERVE AT VTVM2 GET filename filetype APASD-L
*
*   Type the following command, at the "ready prompt," if you are using a VAX system:
*
*       SEND/REMOTE LISTSERV@VTVM2 GET filename filetype APASD-L
*
*   At other BITNET sites, or if these commands fail, contact your local computer center for
*   assistance in determining the proper command syntax. If you are not at a BITNET site,
*   or if you are unable to determine the proper command syntax, send an e-mail message
*   to APASDKLH@GWUVM or APASDSSW@GWUVM requesting the file(s) you want,
*   including a comment that your site cannot send an appropriate command. Science
*   Directorate staff will mail the file(s) to you, usually within a day.
*************************************************************************************

FIGURE 3.6. Index of APA Science Directorate Funding Bulletin Files

| FILENAME | FILETYPE | POSTING DATE | FILE CONTENTS |
|---|---|---|---|
| NIAAA | CENTERS | 07/11/89 | Alcohol Research Center Grants |
| AIDS | MEASURE | 07/11/89 | Measurement, Course, Treatment of HIV |
| AIDS | INDIVIDU | 07/11/89 | Nat. Research Service Awards-Individual |
| AIDS | INSTITU | 07/11/89 | Nat. Research Service Awards-Institutions |
| AIDS | HIV | 07/11/89 | Behavioral & Neurological Aspects of HIV |
| AIDS | NEURO | 07/11/89 | Central Nervous System Effects of HIV |
| NSF | ANNOUNCE | 06/20/89 | NSF Program Announcements** |
| DOD | URI | 06/20/89 | DOD-University Research Initiative** |
| AIDS | MENTILL | 06/20/89 | Mentally Ill at Risk of HIV Infection |
| NIA | RETARDED | 06/20/89 | The Aging of Retarded Adults |
| NIOSH | SERCA | 06/02/89 | Career Award in Occupational Safety |
| NIA | REHAB | 06/02/89 | Rehab. & Aging-Biomedical & Psychosocial |
| AFOSR | SPACE | 06/02/89 | AFOSR-Spatial Orientation Program |
| NIEHS | GRANTS | 06/02/89 | Environmental Health Sciences Grants |
| NCI | FELLOW | 06/02/89 | Cancer Prevention Fellowship Program |
| AIDS | CHILD | 06/02/89 | Children's Knowledge & Emotions about AIDS |
| DRR | ANIMAL | 06/02/89 | Developing & Improving Animal Resources |
| NIMH | ADOLESC | 06/02/89 | Epidemiologic Surveys in Child & Adol. Pop |
| NIH | GUIDE | 05/04/89 | NIH Extramural Programs Guide |
| NIA | CONTROL | 05/04/89 | Sense of Control over the Life Course |
| NIDR | ORALMOTO | 05/04/89 | Normal and Impaired Oral-Motor Function |
| NICHD | AIDS | 05/04/89 | Children's Knowledge/Emotions about AIDS |
| NIMH | EPIDEMIO | 05/04/89 | Mental Disorders Co-Occur Alcohol/Drug |
| NIAAA | MATCHTRE | 05/04/89 | Matching Clients to Treatments |
| NEH | FELLOW | 04/14/89 | National Endowment for the Humanities Fell. |
| NCI | NATIVEAM | 04/14/89 | Avoidable Cancer Mortality in Native Amer. |
| AMFAR | GRANTS | 04/14/89 | American Foundation for AIDS Research |
| AARP | FOUNDA | 04/14/89 | AARPA Andrus Foundation-University Grants |
| NEURO | GRANTS | 04/14/89 | Whitehall Foundation-Grants-in-Aid |
| IWK | FELLOWSH | 04/14/89 | Montreal Neurological Institute Fellowships |
| NSF | TECHCEN | 04/14/89 | NSF Science & Technology Research Centers |
| SCIDIR | CONFER | 04/14/89 | Science Directorate Funds Research Conf. |
| NIH | HUMAN | 04/14/89 | Workshops on Protection of Human Subjects |
| NIA | HUMANFAC | 04/14/89 | Human Factors Research on Older People |
| NIA | INJURIES | 04/14/89 | Reducing Frailty & Injuries in Older Person |
| NIAAA | WARNING | 04/14/89 | Measuring Impact of Alcohol Warning Labels |
| NIMH | MINORITY | 04/14/89 | Minority Mental Health Research Centers |
| ONR | RESDEV | 04/14/89 | ONR-Research & Development Program |
| CDC | INJURY | 04/14/89 | Injury Prevention & Control Research |
| CDC | INJURCEN | 04/14/89 | Injury Prevention Research Centers |
| NIH | ANIMAL | 04/3/89 | Regional Workshops on Care of Animals |
| NICHD | MENRET | 04/3/89 | Mental Retardation Research Centers |
| NHLBI | CHOLEST | 04/3/89 | Lowering Elevated Lipids by Diet |
| APHIS | REGS | 04/3/89 | APHIS Regulations Released-Comments Needed |
| NIA | ALZHEIME | 03/14/89 | Alzheimer's Disease Award for Excellence |
| NIA | ADCARE | 03/14/89 | Alzheimer's Disease: Issues in Caregiving |
| NIMH | ALCOHOL | 03/14/89 | Alcohol, Drug Abuse and Mental Disorders |
| NIMH | SERVICES | 03/14/89 | Services for Severely Mentally Ill Persons |
| NIAAA | SOCIOECO | 03/14/89 | Economic & Socioeconomic Issues of Alcohol |

FIGURE 3.7.  The American Psychological Association Science
Directorate Funding Bulletin Grant Notice

$\rightarrow$
* * * Top of File * * *
00000
00001      MARCH OF DIMES BIRTH DEFECTS FOUNDATION
00002      1275 Mamaroneck Avenue
00003      White Plains, NY 10605
00004      (914) 428-7100
00005      ATTN.: Grants Administration Office
00006
00007      Deadline Date: September 1, 1989
00008
00009      Social & Behavioral Sciences Research: Support is for research
00010      proposals which are interdisciplinary in nature, preferably conducted by
00011      co-investigatorships of physicians and psychologists and focused on the
00012      cognitive development of low birth-weight infants within the first 3
00013      years of life. Grant period begins March 1, 1990.
* * * End of File * * *

Spreadsheet programs usually allow the computer user to print reports and to read information from and write information to other media, primarily disks. The latter feature means data can be interchanged between the spreadsheet program and other programs that use the same data. For example, parts of reports can be prepared using a spreadsheet program and then inserted into a word-processing program, a technique that is used often in responding to an RFP.

The classic use of spreadsheets is for financial management, which includes budget preparation and accounting. The great appeal of spreadsheet programs is that once the relationships among the

TABLE 3.2.   Examples of Spreadsheet Formulas

| Formula | Description |
| --- | --- |
| B1! × 100 | Take what is in cell B1, multiply it by 100, and place the result in the cell where this formula is. |
| @SUM(B1. . .B100) | Add the numbers in Column B, Rows 1 to 100, and place the result in the cell where the formula is. |
| @LOOKUP(B1,E1. . .E20) | Find the largest value in E1 to E20 that is less than or equal to the value in B1; place the contents of the corresponding row in column F in the cell where the formula is. |

data are configured, a change in one element is almost instantly reflected in all other elements that depend in some way on what was changed. For instance, you can view changes in running totals or percentages as you change budget items. Spreadsheets can help in many aspects of research management, such as salary negotiations (e.g., the effect on the project's budget of proposed changes in staff members' salaries can be shown quickly), financial accounting, and maintaining transportation logs. Figure 3.8 uses *Microsoft Excel®* 2.2 to show the research budget for our research on the problem-solving strategies of children. Note that the somewhat abbreviated position descriptions in Column A could have appeared more fully if we chose, or we could have edited them in a word processor so as to be more meaningful. The important point is that the information, once in the spreadsheet, does not have to be retyped for other applications; it can be transferred with a few easy steps.

Many spreadsheets enable the user to display data as graphic presentations such as bar, pie, and line charts. Figure 3.9 shows a bar chart of the distribution of funds for the research budget of our sample study, produced with *Microsoft Excel* 2.2.

FIGURE 3.8. Example of the Problem-Solving Study Research Budget in *Microsoft Excel* 2.2 (Macintosh)

| | A | B | C | D | E | F | G | H | |
|---|---|---|---|---|---|---|---|---|---|
| 7 | Evaluator | 32,600.00 | 0.05 | 1,630.00 | 0.248 | 404.24 | 2,034.24 | 34,230.00 | |
| 8 | Consult | 64,500.00 | 0.02 | 1,290.00 | 0.24 | 309.60 | 1,599.60 | 67,725.00 | |
| 9 | Consult | 53,350.00 | 0.02 | 1,067.00 | 0.24 | 640.20 | 1,707.20 | 56,017.50 | |
| 10 | RA (LRC) | 18,375.00 | 1.00 | 18,375.00 | 0.16 | 2,940.00 | 21,315.00 | 19,293.75 | |
| 11 | RA (LRC) | 18,375.00 | 1.00 | 18,375.00 | 0.16 | 2,940.00 | 21,315.00 | 19,293.75 | |
| 12 | Programmer | 33,360.00 | 0.25 | 8,340.00 | 0.248 | 2,068.32 | 10,408.32 | 35,028.00 | |
| 13 | Office Asst. | 10,206.00 | 0.25 | 2,551.50 | 0.248 | 632.77 | 3,184.27 | 10,818.36 | |
| 14 | | | | | | | | | |
| 15 | | | Int. Sub | 64,564.11 | | 13,089.28 | | | |
| 16 | | | | | | | | | |
| 17 | Computer Equipment | | | | | | 38,858.00 | | |
| 18 | Domestic Travel | | | | | | 2,000.00 | | |
| 19 | | | | | | | | | |
| 20 | | | Subtotals | | | | 118,511.39 | | |
| 21 | | | | | | | | | |
| 22 | | | | | | | | | |
| 23 | | | Total | | | | 118,511.39 | | |
| 24 | | | | | | | | | |
| 25 | | | | | | | | | |
| 26 | Project Totals | | | Computer Equipment | | | | | |
| 27 | | | | | | | | | |
| 28 | Salaries & Wages | 129,907.09 | | Description | | | Price | Quantity | Amc |
| 29 | Fringes | 25,842.06 | | | | | | | |
| 30 | Computer Equip. | 38,858.00 | | PS/2 Model 30 286 HD Bundle | | | 2,570.00 | 9 | 2 |
| 31 | Travel | 4,000.00 | | PS/2 Model 70 HD 60 | | | 3,235.00 | 3 | |
| 32 | 2 YR Total | 198,607.15 | | Hi-Res Color Monitor | | | 1,005.00 | 3 | |
| 33 | | | | Proprinter III | | | 475.00 | 5 | |
| 34 | | | | IBM PS/2 Mouse | | | 72.00 | 3 | |
| 35 | By Year Total | 198,607.15 | | DOS 4.0 3.5" | | | 94.00 | 3 | |
| 36 | | | | Microsoft Windows 286 | | | 45.00 | 3 | |
| 37 | | | | | | | | | |
| 38 | | | | | | | | Total | 3 |
| 39 | | | | | | | | | |

FIGURE 3.9. Graphic for the Problem-Solving Study Budget
Produced Using *Microsoft Excel 2.2*

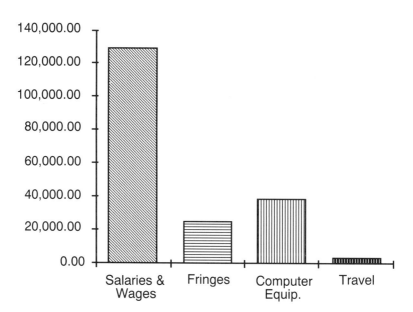

Two features of the spreadsheet are especially attractive to project managers. The first allows the planner to ask "what if" questions. For example, "what if" staff salaries go up 5% next year? Or "what if" overhead rates increase 6%? Most public universities attach overhead to sponsored projects or grants as a way to recoup resources expended during the course of the project (e.g., equipment, supplies, utilities, etc.). Furthermore, many universities make a distinction between different types of sponsors—a state grant might be assigned a different overhead rate than a corporate-sponsored grant. Using spreadsheet software, a researcher can calculate a budget with differential overhead rates easily. And since all relationships are defined, changing any item automatically changes all other items related to it .

A second major advantage of a spreadsheet is that once one budget has been planned, it usually can be used as a template for other budgets, so that eventually the researcher will have a set of "standard" budgets to use in a variety of grant situations (e.g., one template for training grants, another for federal research grants, etc.). Many university offices of sponsored projects even will provide a template or help you set up one. It is in their interest to do so because

## Spreadsheet Software

| Apple Family | Apple Macintosh | IBM PC |
|---|---|---|
| AppleWorks<br>Claris Corp.<br>5201 Patrick Henry Dr.<br>P.O. Box 58168<br>Santa Clara, CA 95052<br>(800)544-8554 | Microsoft Excel<br>Microsoft Corporation<br>16011 NE 36th Way<br>Box 97017<br>Redmond, WA 98073<br>(800)426-9400 | Microsoft Excel<br>Microsoft Corporation<br>16011 NE 36th Way<br>Box 97017<br>Redmond, WA 98073<br>(800)426-9400 |
| VisiCalc for the PC<br>IBM Corp., Applications<br>Systems Division<br>472 Wheeler Farms Rd.<br>Milford, CT 06460<br>(203)783-7000 | WingZ<br>Informix Software<br>16011 College Blvd.<br>Lenexa, KS 66219<br>(913)492-3800 | Lotus 123<br>Lotus Development Corp.<br>55 Cambridge Parkway<br>Cambridge, MA 02142<br>(617)577-8500 |
| SuperCalc<br>Computer Associates<br>International Inc.<br>1240 McKay Drive<br>San Jose, CA 95131<br>(800)531-5236 | Full Impact<br>Ashton-Tate<br>20101 Hamilton Ave.<br>Torrance, CA 90502<br>(213)329-8000 | Quattro<br>Borland International<br>1800 Green Hill Road<br>Scotts Valley, CA 95066<br>(408)438-8400 |
| MagiCalc<br>ArtSci, Inc.<br>P.O. Box 1848<br>Burbank, CA 91505<br>(818)843-4080 | Trapeze<br>Access Technology, Inc.<br>200G Heritage Harbor<br>Monterey, CA 93940<br>(800)367-4334 | SuperCalc<br>Computer Associates<br>International, Inc.<br>1240 McKay Drive<br>San Jose, CA 95131<br>(800)531-5236 |

they will have more confidence in the numbers you provide and can check your figures more easily.

Finally, spreadsheets are quite useful for data entry later on in the research cycle. Many statistical analysis packages will accept data created by spreadsheets if they are stored as ASCII text files.

### Project Management

Spreadsheets tend to approach the calculation of income and expenses from an microanalytical point of view. For example, a spreadsheet on the expense of sending out a self-completed mail questionnaire would calculate the sum of the costs for paper, printing, postage, and follow-up phone calls. However, the self-completed mail questionnaire is but one of many tasks in the research cycle, and obviously one must "cost out" the entire study by examining all the other tasks (jobs) involved. This is the function of project-management software. Project-management software keeps track of all resources, time, and costs relative to a project.

Using project-management software to aid in planning a study has a number of advantages. First, the project-management software offers an administrator at least three perspectives in planning a project: (1) the activities necessary to get the job done, (2) allocation of resources to accomplish the task, and (3) a time frame to complete the work. We examine each perspective individually below.

The activities required to get the job done basically are outlined from the tasks listed in the "Research Cycle." Each of these tasks may be broken into subtasks to give a clearer picture of the processes involved. For example, in our proposed study on problem-solving strategies, we might plan on going through standard steps such as getting permission from the location where the study is to be conducted, going through a human-subjects review, pilot testing the instrument, collecting data, and so on. Somewhere along the way, we might have to specify the development of a computer program to collect the information (instrument development), if this is how we intend to collect data for the study. Figure 3.10 illustrates a task specification for our hypothetical research project.

Planning the allocation of resources enables the researcher to determine whether funds will be available when they are needed for

FIGURE 3.10. *MacProject* II Task View of Some Steps in the Problem-Solving Research Study (Macintosh)

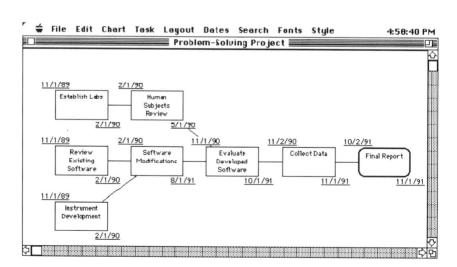

each job. The coordinated allocation of resources also prevents delays and helps ensure that the project staff will be paid on time.

Formulating a time frame within which work must be completed requires consideration of a number of variables. The first variable, of course, is how long it will take to physically do the job. For example, if you use a self-completed mail survey in the United States, you can expect that it will take at least two weeks to get a return on the first wave of data collection—one to five days for your survey to reach its destination and three to five days for it to be completed and returned. Most self-completed mail surveys incorporate three waves of data collection—an initial mail-out and two follow-ups for non-responders. Essentially, this means a minimum of six weeks from start to finish. Other variables, however, can affect this estimate. For example, if you are using students or temporary staff to print forms, stuff envelopes, and mail questionnaires, you must take into consideration their availability. You also should assess the availability of the intended target population. Sending out a survey in mid-November may not be productive because so many people are absent during the holiday season. Project-management software can help you resolve the problems of multiple schedules and ask "what if" questions to assess the impact of delays. Your goal is to find a "critical path" among the various activities and monitor that path carefully. Figure 3.11 illustrates a timeline of the activities involved in conducting our hypothetical research study.

FIGURE 3.11.   *MacProject* II Timeline View of the Proposed
Problem-Solving Research Study (Macintosh)

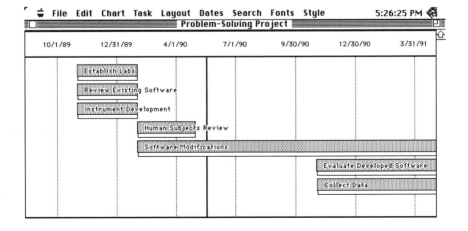

## Project-Management Software

| Apple Family | Apple Macintosh | IBM PC |
|---|---|---|
| VisiSchedule<br>VisiCorp Software Corp.<br>1616 Randolph Pkwy.<br>Los Altos, CA 94022<br>(415)964-4657 | MacProject II<br>Claris Corp.<br>5201 Patrick Henry Dr.<br>P.O. Box 58168<br>Santa Clara, CA 95052<br>(800)544-8554 | Harvard Total Project<br>Manager II<br>Software Publishing Corp.<br>P.O. Box 7210<br>1901 Landings Dr.<br>Mountain View, CA 94039<br>(415)962-8910 |
| Project Planner<br>Applitech Software, Inc.<br>381 Harvard St.<br>Cambridge, MA 02138<br>(617)497-8268 | Great Gantt<br>Varcon Systems, Inc<br>10509 San Diego Mission<br>Road, Suite K<br>San Diego, CA 92108<br>(619)563-6700 | Microsoft Project<br>Microsoft Corporation<br>16011 NE 36th Way<br>Box 97017<br>Redmond, WA 98073<br>(800)426-9400 |
| Everybody's Planner<br>Abracadata, Inc.<br>P.O. Box 2440<br>Eugene, OR 97402<br>(503)342-3030 | FastTrack Schedule<br>AEC Management Systems<br>Inc.<br>22611 Markey Court,<br>Building 113<br>Sterling, VA 22170<br>(800)346-9413 | Time Line<br>Symantec Corp.<br>10201 Torre Ave.<br>Cupertino, CA 95014<br>(800)441-7234<br>(800)626-8847 in CA |
| Critical Path Analysis<br>Sourceview Software Intl.<br>P.O. Box 578<br>Concord, CA 94522-0578<br>(415)686-8439 | MacSchedule<br>Mainstay<br>5311-B Derry Drive<br>Agoura Hills, CA 91301<br>(818)991-6540 | VP-Planner Plus<br>Paperback Software<br>2830 Ninth St.<br>Berkeley, CA 94710<br>(415)644-2116 |
| PERT Program Evaluation &<br>Review Technique<br>National Collegiate<br>Software Clearinghouse<br>Duke University Press<br>6697 College Station<br>Durham, NC 27708<br>(919)737-3067 | Key Plan<br>Symmetry Software Corp.<br>225 E. First St.<br>Mesa, AZ 85203<br>(602)844-2199 | InstaPlan<br>InstaPlan Corp.<br>655 Redwood Highway,<br>Suite 311<br>Mill Valley, CA 94941<br>(800)852-7526 |

## Word Processing

Word processing is the most ubiquitous of all software applications. With a little imagination, a word processor can be used on just about every step of the research cycle. Because word processing comes into play so often and is so useful, we describe it briefly here.

Word processors have become quite sophisticated. They fall into two main categories. The first, "what you see is what you get" (or WYSIWYG, pronounced "wizzy-wig") is just that: What you see on the screen is what gets printed on paper. For example, the line of text shown on the terminal screen in Figure 3.12 would look on paper just as it does on the screen.

The second category of word processing is defined by its use of embedded commands. For example, the first line shown on the word-processing screen in Figure 3.13 is an *embedded command*. If the word-processing program were to print the screen, the printed document would look like that shown in Figure 3.12. The embedded commands give printing directions and are displayed on the screen, but they are not printed by the printer.

Your first reaction might be to say that WYSIWYG word processing is more natural and easier to learn. True, but the reason embedded-command word processing is still popular is that it offers more power and flexibility. It is harder to learn, but, once having mastered it, the user can alter the margins and spacing and make other changes without reformatting the entire document. Nevertheless, WYSIWYG word processing is almost as powerful, and we predict that eventually it will replace embedded commands in word processing.

The most basic functions of every word processor are performed by three commands: Delete, Copy, and Move. These three

FIGURE 3.12. Example of a WYSIWYG Word Processor in *Microsoft Word* 4.0 (Macintosh)

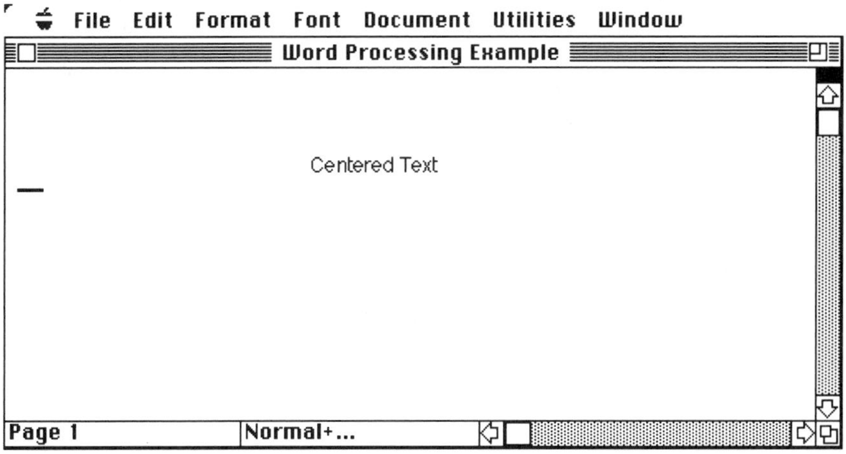

FIGURE 3.13.  Example of a Word Processor that Uses
Embedded Commands

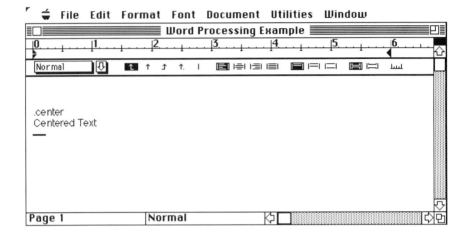

commands demonstrate the basic power and convenience of word processing.

*Delete.*  Many word processors allow you to delete in both forward or backward directions. Deleting backward corresponds to the so-called self-correcting typewriters that allow you to backspace one character and remove the character by printing over it with correction tape. However, most word processors allow you to delete not only one character, but words, lines, or entire paragraphs or sections. Figure 3.14 illustrates the use of highlighting a portion of text to be deleted in *Microsoft Word*® 4.0, a popular word-processing package for both MS-DOS and Macintosh machines. After the text is highlighted, a keystroke combination from the keyboard or a menu selection will delete the block.

*Copy and Move.*  These commands are very similar to each other. With each, you mark or highlight a portion of text. You can then move the text to a point designated by the cursor, or you can simply copy the marked text without removing it from its original position. Figures 3.15 and 3.16 show a two-step process of moving a block of text. In the first step, the block of text is highlighted. In the second step, a place in the document is selected as the insertion

FIGURE 3.14.  DELETE command in *Microsoft Word* 4.0 on
Macintosh (highlighted text will be deleted)

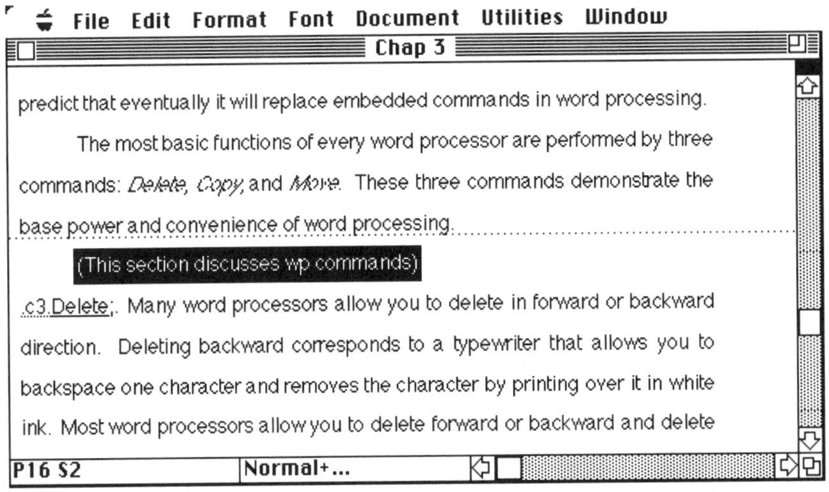

```
  r  ⬥  File   Edit   Format   Font   Document   Utilities   Window
 ▤▢▬▬▬▬▬▬▬▬▬▬▬▬▬▬▬▬▬ Chap 3 ▬▬▬▬▬▬▬▬▬▬▬▬▬▬▬▬▬▬▬▫▤

   predict that eventually it will replace embedded commands in word processing.        ⬆
          The most basic functions of every word processor are performed by three
   commands: *Delete, Copy,* and *Move.* These three commands demonstrate the
   base power and convenience of word processing.
        (This section discusses wp commands)
   .c3.Delete;. Many word processors allow you to delete in forward or backward
   direction.  Deleting backward corresponds to a typewriter that allows you to
   backspace one character and removes the character by printing over it in white
   ink. Most word processors allow you to delete forward or backward and delete    ⬇
 ▤P16 S2                    │Normal+...          │◁▢▒▒▒▒▒▒▒▒▒▒▒▒▒▒▒▒▷▫
```

FIGURE 3.15.  Part 1 of MOVE command in *Microsoft Word* 4.0
(highlighted text will be moved)

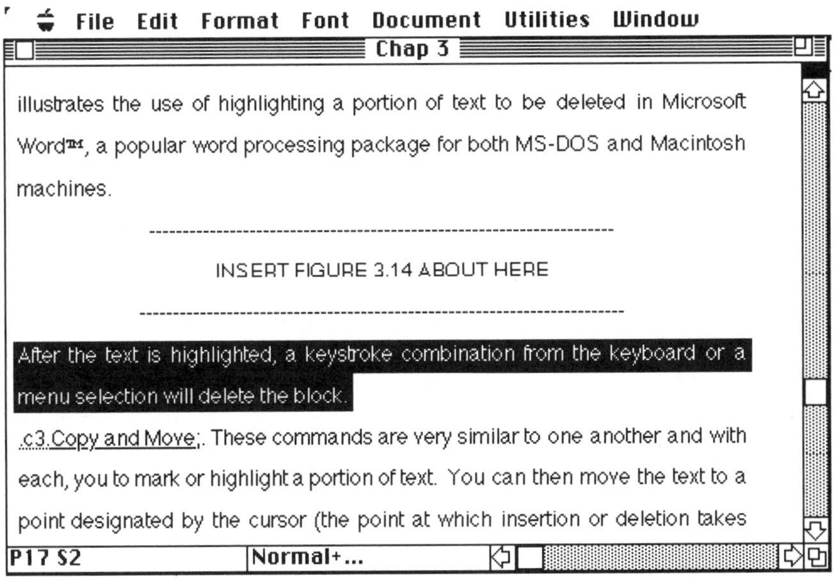

```
  r  ⬥  File   Edit   Format   Font   Document   Utilities   Window
 ▤▢▬▬▬▬▬▬▬▬▬▬▬▬▬▬▬▬▬ Chap 3 ▬▬▬▬▬▬▬▬▬▬▬▬▬▬▬▬▬▬▬▫▤

   illustrates the use of highlighting a portion of text to be deleted in Microsoft   ⬆
   Word™, a popular word processing package for both MS-DOS and Macintosh
   machines.

            ------------------------------------------------------------
                     INSERT FIGURE 3.14 ABOUT HERE
            ------------------------------------------------------------

   After the text is highlighted, a keystroke combination from the keyboard or a
   menu selection will delete the block.
   .c3.Copy and Move;. These commands are very similar to one another and with
   each, you to mark or highlight a portion of text. You can then move the text to a
   point designated by the cursor (the point at which insertion or deletion takes   ⬇
 ▤P17 S2                    │Normal+...          │◁▢▒▒▒▒▒▒▒▒▒▒▒▒▒▒▒▒▷▫
```

FIGURE 3.16. Part 2 of MOVE command in *Microsoft Word* 4.0
(text has been moved)

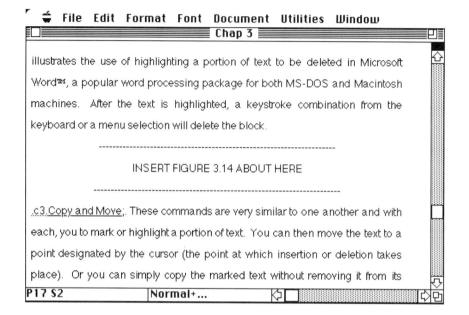

point. A keystroke combination from the keyboard or a menu selection completes the move.

*Search and Replace.* Another useful feature of most word processors is the global search-and-replace function. This function directs the computer to search through a stored document for a given word or phrase and, at the user's option, replace it with something else. This is very convenient for updating a document and is a built-in feature of almost every spellchecker. It will save you work in other ways, too. For example, a large word or phrase that will appear often in a document can be abbreviated in working drafts, then changed to its complete form throughout the entire document in the final version. For instance, you could type "ASA" throughout your working draft, then change this globally to "American Statistical Association" when the document is finished. Figure 3.17 shows an example of a search-and-change option in *Microsoft Word* 4.0.

For a more detailed discussion of word processing, the reader may wish to consult Lombardi (1988) or Assadi (1989).

The convenience of word processing in the formative stages of

FIGURE 3.17. Search and Replace

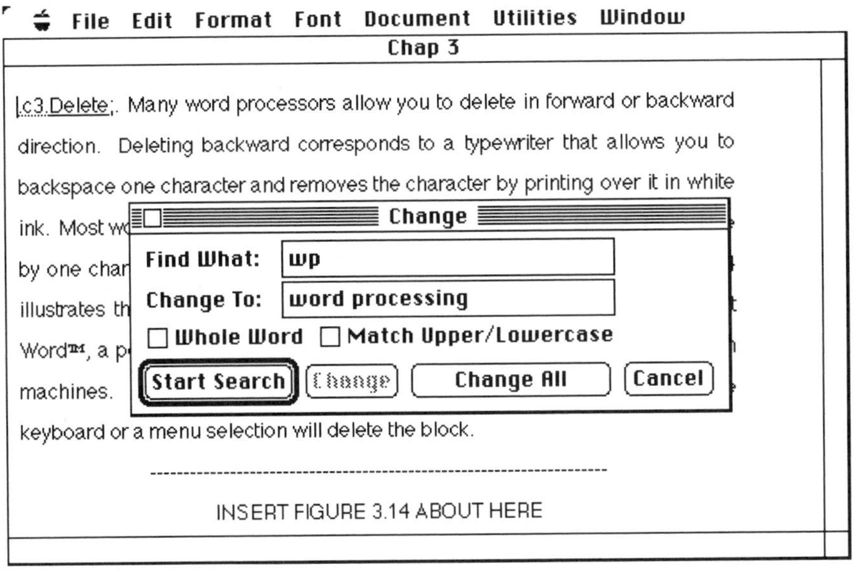

**File  Edit  Format  Font  Document  Utilities  Window**

### Chap 3

|c3.Delete;. Many word processors allow you to delete in forward or backward direction. Deleting backward corresponds to a typewriter that allows you to backspace one character and removes the character by printing over it in white ink. Most w

**Change**

**Find What:** wp

**Change To:** word processing

☐ Whole Word  ☐ Match Upper/Lowercase

[ **Start Search** ]  [ Change ]  [ **Change All** ]  [ **Cancel** ]

by one char
illustrates th
Word™, a p
machines.

keyboard or a menu selection will delete the block.

------------------------------------------------------------------

INSERT FIGURE 3.14 ABOUT HERE

developing a proposal results from the ease with which one can revise. We often pass around several printed versions (referred to as "hard copy") of a proposal so that the proposal reviewers and developers can make direct comments in pen. (Yes, there is still a place for pens, although some researchers do pass around the document stored on floppy disks.*) One person gathers all the comments and then uses a word processor to revise and edit the final document. This procedure saves hours of retyping and revising. It increases our productivity by speeding up the process and improves the quality of the final document because our attention is focused on writing and not on text editing.

In view of the revisions that are necessary in written instruments such as questionnaires and procedures, the ease with which a

---

*There are now applications which permit workgroup editing and review. *Mark-Up*, for example, allows group members to edit any type of Macintosh document without having the application that created it. It is based on a metaphor of mark-ups on a set of transparent overlays of an original document. Tools are provided for each group member to edit and mark up a separate layer over the document. *MarkUp* is a trademark of Mainstay, 5311-B Derry Ave., Agoura Hills, CA 91301. Phone: (818)991-6540.

document can be modified is a blessing (although admittedly it probably leads us to make more changes than necessary).

## Use of Templates

Often there are cases in grant or research proposal writing that call for the same passages to be used in more than one proposal, either verbatim or with only slight modifications. For example, each proposal could include the same descriptions of work, research facilities, qualifications and background of researchers, and so on. Using templates, the grant writer can save considerable time by loading the

### Word-Processing Software

| Apple Family | Apple Macintosh | IBM PC |
|---|---|---|
| AppleWorks<br>Claris Corp.<br>5201 Patrick Henry Dr.<br>P.O. Box 58168<br>Santa Clara, CA 95052<br>(800)544-8554 | Microsoft Word<br>Microsoft Corporation<br>16011 NE 36th Way<br>Box 97017<br>Redmond, WA 98073<br>(800)426-9400 | Microsoft Word<br>Microsoft Corporation<br>16011 NE 36th Way<br>Box 97017<br>Redmond, WA 98073<br>(800)426-9400 |
| Word Perfect for the Apple<br>IIE/IIC<br>WordPerfect Corp.<br>1555 N. Technology Way<br>Orem, UT 84057<br>(801)225-5000 | MacWrite II<br>Claris Corp.<br>5201 Patrick Henry Dr.<br>P.O. Box 58168<br>Santa Clara, CA 95052<br>(800)544-8554 | WordPerfect<br>WordPerfect Corporation<br>1555 N. Technology Way<br>Orem, UT 84057<br>(801)225-5000 |
| Multiscribe<br>Styleware, Inc.<br>440 Clyde Ave.<br>Mountain View, CA 94043<br>(415)960-1500 | FullWrite Professional<br>Ashton-Tate<br>20101 Hamilton Ave.<br>Torrance, CA 90502<br>(213)329-8000 | Multimate Advantage II<br>Ashton-Tate<br>20101 Hamilton Ave.<br>Torrance, CA 90502<br>(213)329-8000 |
| PFS-Write<br>Scholastic, Inc.<br>P.O. Box 7502<br>2931 E. McCarty St.<br>Jefferson City, MO 65102<br>(800)541-5513 | WriteNow for the Macintosh<br>T/Maker Co.<br>1390 Villa St.<br>Mountain View, CA 94041<br>(415)962-0195 | WordStar Professional<br>Micropro International Corp.<br>33 San Pablo Ave.<br>San Rafael, CA 94903<br>(800)227-5609 |
| Magic Window II<br>ArtSci, Inc.<br>P.O. Box 1848<br>Burbank, CA 91505<br>(818)843-4080 | Nisus<br>Paragon Concepts, Inc.<br>990 Highland Dr., Ste. 312<br>Solana Beach, CA 92075<br>(619)481-1477 | Samna Word IV<br>Samna Corp.<br>5600 Glenridge Dr.<br>Atlanta, GA 30342<br>(800)831-9679 |

same text from a common file into each unique document. He or she can also produce several variations of the same document by trying out different approaches and then "pasting together" the final version.

### Spelling, Word Usage, Grammar, Punctuation, and Style Checkers

There are systems that can read your document and check it for common spelling, grammar, and style errors. The spellchecker compares each word in your document against a dictionary. If it spots something "wrong," it points out the word so that you can mark, change, or ignore it. Most spellcheckers allow you to compile your own dictionary, which is useful for words unique to your field or for proper names. Alternatively, you can simply instruct the program to ignore the word and continue checking your document. Some spellcheckers will even suggest words they think you are trying to spell. Unless your spelling of the word is badly mangled, the checker tends to "guess" correctly 70–80% of the time. Many word-processing packages have spellcheckers built in.

Another useful word-processing tool is the electronic thesaurus. It works much like the book found on many writers' desks, except that it usually is much more convenient to use and generally more extensive. The way the thesaurus typically works is that you highlight the word or phrase you'd like to change and ask the thesaurus to display a list of synonyms. Once you've found an alternative word that you like, most programs allow you to simply highlight the alternative and then transfer it to your document by a keystroke combination from the keyboard or a menu selection. Figure 3.18 illustrates the thesaurus function of *Spelling Coach*™ *Professional*, a popular word usage tool for the Macintosh computer.

At present grammar- and style-checking programs are less helpful than spelling and word-usage checkers. The level of sophistication in artificial intelligence as applied to languages makes it difficult for a computer to check grammar and style. Programs usually work on the technique of looking for the most common "errors." For example, some programs judge use of the word *upon* as "archaic usage"; the checker might suggest using *on* instead. In another example, the program might judge the phrase *until such time as* wordy and suggest that you substitute *until*. Often these "errors" are more a question of preference or style, but the computer's exhortations generally are useful enough to warrant paying attention to them. Figure 3.19 displays the style- and grammar-checking features of Mac-Proof™, a handy software program for the Macintosh computer.

FIGURE 3.18.  Example of a Thesaurus in *Coach Professional*
3.0 by Deneba Software (Macintosh)

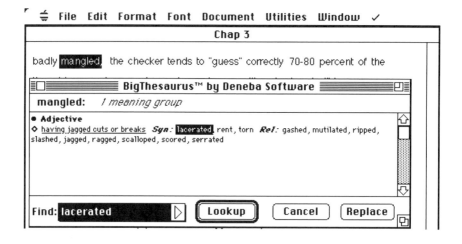

FIGURE 3.19.  Example of Style-Checking Function of *MacProof*
3.0 (suspected errors are highlighted)

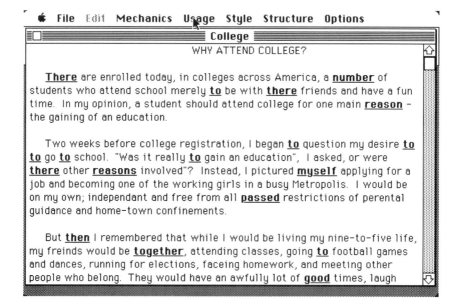

## Style, Word-Usage, and Spellchecking Software

| Apple Family | Apple Macintosh | IBM PC |
|---|---|---|
| Sensible Speller IV<br>Sensible Software, Inc.<br>335 E. Big Beaver, Ste. 207<br>Troy, MI 48083<br>(313)528-1950 | Grammatik Mac<br>Reference Software<br>330 Townsend St.,<br>Suite 123<br>San Francisio, CA 94107<br>(415)541-0222 | Grammatik III<br>Reference Software<br>330 Townsend St.<br>Suite 123<br>San Francisio, CA 94107<br>(415)541-0222 |
| Sensible Grammar<br>Sensible Software, Inc.<br>335 E. Big Beaver, Ste. 207<br>Troy, MI 48083<br>(313)528-1950 | Doug Clapp's Word Tools<br>Aegis Development, Inc.<br>2115 Pico Blvd.<br>Santa Monica, CA 90405<br>(213)392-9972 | Right Writer<br>Rightsoft Inc.<br>2033 Wood St., Ste. 218<br>Sarasota, FL 33577<br>(813)952-9211 |
| AppleWorks Timeout Series<br>Beagle Brothers<br>6215 Serris Sq., Ste. 100<br>San Diego, CA 92121<br>(800)345-1750<br>(800)992-4022 in CA | Coach Professional<br>Deneba Software<br>3305 N.W. 74th Ave.<br>Miami, FL 33122<br>(305)594-6965 | Electric Webster<br>Cornucopia Software Inc.<br>P.O. Box 6111<br>Albany, CA 94706<br>(415)524-8098 |
| Fleet System 3<br>Professional Software, Inc.<br>Lakeside Office Park<br>599 North Ave., Door 7<br>Wakefield, MA 01880<br>(617)246-2425 | MacProof<br>Lexpertise USA<br>175 East 400 South<br>Suite 1000<br>Salt Lake City, UT 84111<br>(800)354-5656 | Sensible Grammar<br>Sensible Software, Inc.<br>335 E. Big Beaver, Ste. 207<br>Troy, MI 48083<br>(313)528-1950 |

## Word Processing via Telecommunications

This entire manuscript was managed from The University of Texas at Austin. However, three of the authors, Carl and Paul of the University of Michigan and Ernie of the University of Massachusetts, Amherst, never left their campuses, nor did they physically send their contributions. They produced their manuscript text on microcomputer word processors, then transmitted it via telephone and commercial satellite to the mainframe computer at The University of Texas. The process employed four different microcomputers (three Apples and a PC) to transfer the files to a mainframe. Final editing was done on an Apple Macintosh; an Apple LaserWriter was used for printing the manuscript. We describe this process to alert the reader to the possibilities of collaboration that exist when you combine the technology of word processing with that of telecommunications.

## SUMMARY

The specification of objectives and hypotheses can involve a number of administrative "side steps." Specifically, if you are looking to see whether or not your research can be funded, you might consider grant monitoring via telecommunications. Spreadsheets will help you determine a budget for your study, and project-management software can facilitate the scheduling of the various groups that will be involved in the research. Word processors, in some ways the crux of all your microcomputer activities, can be used for grant writing and many other activities. Finally, there are a number of word tools that can be used to make the writing more professional: spelling, grammar, and style checkers, and the electronic thesaurus. Such software not only can improve the quality of your work, but most likely increase your productivity as well.

# 4

# Planning the Research: Operational

## INTRODUCTION

This chapter introduces programs that can aid the researcher in choosing appropriate statistical techniques, determining the required sample size and its relationship to statistical power, and choosing an efficient research design. These tend to be the most elusive problems in the research process because the researcher often is extending inquiry into areas which are not well developed. The choices generally are concurrent with early steps in the research process (see Table 4.1 and Figure 4.1). As was the case with previous steps in the research cycle, the tasks accomplished here interact with one another. For example, a problem in sample implementation in a survey study might prompt a redefinition of the target population. Alternatively, the problem might suggest that some variables could be excluded or redefined so that the study can be implemented later.

We hope to demonstrate that one can use information from related areas and fields to help make the research plan a rational effort. In many ways, designing the research plan is like designing a bridge. No one has ever built a bridge exactly the way the engineers planned. There is always uncertainty about the result. The engineer must synthesize a number of variables (e.g., bridge expanse, type of soil, etc.) and, on the basis of past knowledge, plan a structure which can meet the constraints imposed by those variables. Similarly, the social science researcher must synthesize relevant variables and, on the basis of accumulated knowledge, plan a study which takes into consideration the restrictions of the variables involved. There are

TABLE 4.1.   Research Matrix for Steps 4 and 2a–4a of the Research Cycle

| Research Task | Application | Use |
|---|---|---|
| **Step 4. Define Operational Plan and Specify Variables** | | |
| Planning Statistical Analyses | Decision-Support Software for Statistical Analysis | Only the appropriate statistical analysis will help us reach our research objectives. Microcomputers can take the researcher through a decision heuristic that guides the user through a series of smaller decision steps that explore the nature of the research question, properties of the data being collected, and statistical assumptions the user is willing to make. |
| Planning the Research Design | Decision-Support Software for Research Designs | Much of the design process is a function of knowing what has transpired in previous studies related to the one the researcher is proposing. Microcomputer software may help the researcher quantify the anticipated effect of a proposed intervention through techniques such as meta-analysis. For experimental designs, software can recommend a design that will achieve the greatest efficiency for the type of question being posed. |
| **Steps 2a, 3a, and 4a. Defining, Specifying, and Implementing Sample-Selection Procedures** | | |
| Planning the Sample-Size Calculation/Power Analysis | Sample-Size Calculation/Power-Analysis Software | Calculating sample size or power is an integral part of the planning process and affects both administrative and operational considerations. Microcomputer software addresses this issue and helps the researcher to make more rational decisions about the size and scope of the proposed study. |

two practical differences between the efforts of structural engineers and social science researchers: (1) engineers work with things, while social scientists work with people; and (2) the variables relevant to the construction of bridges generally are well known, while the variables relevant to a social science study oftentimes must first be identified.

FIGURE 4.1. Issues in Design and Sample Size

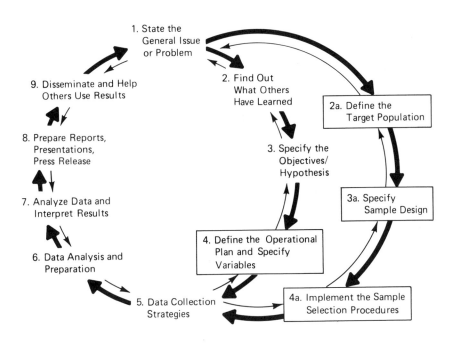

## CHOOSING APPROPRIATE STATISTICS

The first step after posing a research question is to ask, "What evidence or information would allow me to answer this question?" Because of the vast amounts of information gathered in a social science study, most researchers rely on quantitative indices or statistics to help them make decisions. Social science researchers commonly use decision-making trees or statistical guides to help with the selection of appropriate statistics (e.g., Andrews, Klem, Davidson, O'Malley, & Rodgers, 1981; Harshbarger, 1971). Before the researcher can make a choice of statistics, a number of decision components must be considered. How many variables are involved in the analysis? What are their levels of measurement? What assumptions, if any, can be made about the nature of the relationships? Is a statistical test of significance more important than discovering the strength of a relationship? What statistic(s) will communicate most effectively to the intended audience?

Once the statistic or technique has been chosen, the researcher can perform the analysis using any of the numerous microcomputer or mainframe statistical-analysis software packages currently available (e.g., SAS, SPSS-X, Systat®, OSIRIS, etc.).* A major advantage of using a planned approach is that the researcher will know immediately if no statistical technique exists to answer the research question as it is currently framed. For example, a researcher who wants to look at a symmetrical relationship between an intervally scaled and an ordinally scaled variable will find that no statistical technique has been developed to measure the relationship. Typically, the researcher would either (a) assume that the ordinal variable is interval and calculate a Pearson product moment correlation coefficient to characterize the relationship, or (b) assume that variables are ordinal and calculate a Spearman's *rho* correlation coefficient.

This section serves to introduce the development of *HyperStat II*™. Based on *A Guide for Selecting Statistical Techniques for Analyzing Social Science Data* (Andrews et al., 1981), *HyperStat II*† was written to (1) provide an interactive computer-assisted decision model for selecting a particular statistic or statistical technique, and (2) serve as a prototype for other interactive decision models in research and evaluation designs (Shermis, Cole, & Heyden, 1990). The program was developed in *HyperCard*™, a database-programming environment which allows the user to create educational "stackware" by manipulating objects of text or graphics that are stored on electronically simulated "cards." These objects represent "events" that the author wants the computer to produce, such as branching to another card that contains questions or information (Shermis, 1987).

Currently published guides use the notion of linear programming by asking "critical questions" and eliciting one-solution user responses. One disadvantage of most guides is that the user must know how to properly interpret each question as it is posed. Because subsequent decisions are based on previous ones, an error made early in the process compounds rapidly. Another disadvantage is that the user needs to be familiar with a wide variety of statistical terms. Although most guides provide supplemental information, explanations of terms and questions sometimes are not included or require some effort to find.

The program ("stackware") helps select appropriate statistics, and the user usually can solicit help to answer questions before making a decision. In *HyperStat II*, the user has interactive access to short, non-mathematical explanations of technical terms and brief

---

*This presumes that the researcher knows how to use whatever system(s) are
  locally available, and can make appropriate choices among each system.
†Support for the development of the program was provided by the School of
  Nursing and Project Quest, The University of Texas at Austin.

descriptions of key words embedded in a question.* Through familiarization with an interactive computer-based decision model, the user (1) develops a greater knowledge of statistical terms, techniques, and manipulations; and (2) has a greater likelihood of success in selecting a statistic or technique appropriate to analyze a particular set of data.

*HyperStat II* facilitates two decision-making operations. Using it as a heuristic aid, a teacher of research design or statistics can set up a series of hypothetical problems, then have students use the program to select appropriate statistics for subsequent data analysis. For example, a math instructor wished to compare two methods of teaching problem solving. The dependent variable of interest was the number of correct answers on a locally developed test. To control for sex differences, the instructor randomly selected two groups of students, with equal numbers of boys and girls in each group. Because scores on the *Test of Logical Thinking* (Tobin & Capie, 1979) were available for all the students, the instructor wished to use logical thinking ability as a mediating variable.

Students faced with such a problem could consult *HyperStat II* to discover the best analytic strategies, given the constraints of this situation. Figures 4.2 through 4.8 illustrate a *HyperStat II* session by an uninitiated user trying to solve the instructor's problem of what statistical technique to use for analyzing the given data.

*HyperStat II* also serves as a heuristic for problem solving by helping the user systematically investigate a series of possible questions. Advantages of operating in this mode include: (1) the student is able to ask for explanations of unfamiliar terms and techniques; (2) references to statistics or techniques are contained in one program; and (3) the artificial intelligence built into the system helps the researcher ask the "right" questions.

*HyperStat II* also is useful to the experienced researcher or data analyst by helping to formulate an analysis strategy that is based either on a pre-existing design or on knowledge of the limitations with which the researcher is faced. For instance, the illustration above could be either a teacher's instructional example or a "real-world" problem. In the latter case, the researcher obtains one possible solution in a systematic way. However, we advise experimentation with the different "branches of the tree," especially to explore what impact might be exerted on the data analysis by different assumptions about the statistics or the level and type of measurement.

---

*\*HyperStat II* provides quick references for techniques, concepts, or terms which may require more in-depth explanation. The information is controlled by the user and is available "on demand" for capitalized words.

FIGURE 4.2.  Opening Screen for *HyperStat* II
(Macintosh)—''>2'' Selected

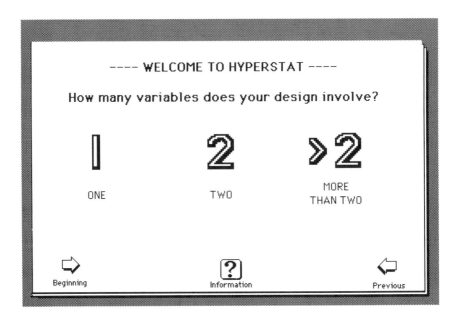

FIGURE 4.3.  *HyperStat* II—''Yes'' Selected

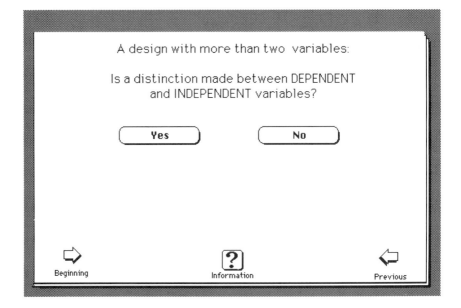

FIGURE 4.4. *HyperStat* II—"No" Selected

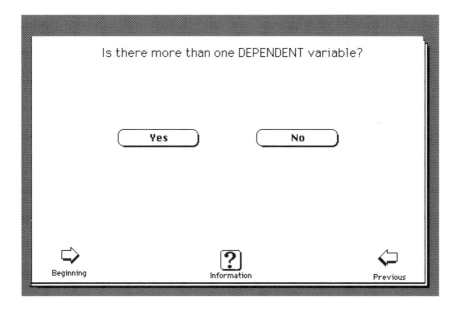

FIGURE 4.5. *HyperStat* II—"Yes" Selected

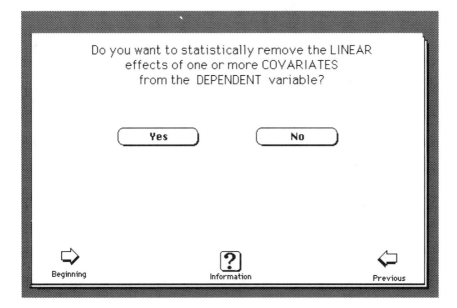

FIGURE 4.6.  *HyperStat* II—''Yes'' Selected

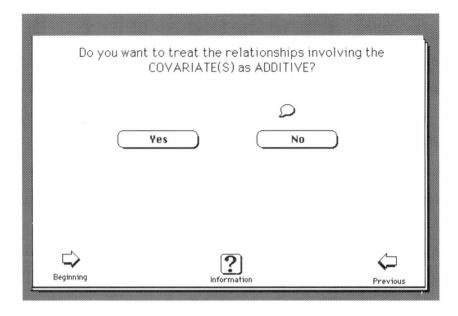

FIGURE 4.7.  *HyperStat* II—''Yes'' Selected

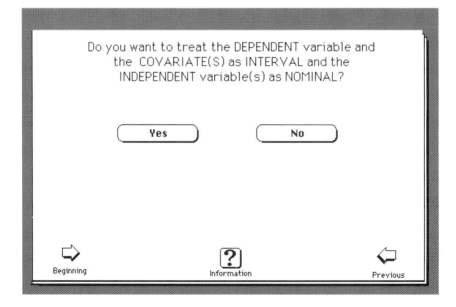

FIGURE 4.8. *HyperStat* II—Recommended Statistical Analysis Test

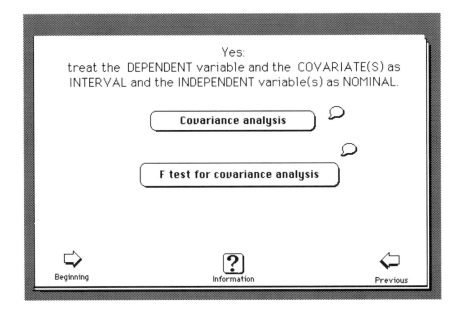

## Choosing Statistics

| Apple Family | Apple Macintosh | IBM PC |
|---|---|---|
| Which Statistic?<br>National Collegiate<br>Software Clearinghouse<br>Duke University Press<br>6697 College Station<br>Durham, NC 27708<br>(919)737-3067 | Which Statistic?<br>National Collegiate<br>Software Clearinghouse<br>Duke University Press<br>6697 College Station<br>Durham, NC 27708<br>(919)737-3067 | Which Statistic?<br>National Collegiate<br>Software Clearinghouse<br>Duke University Press<br>6697 College Station<br>Durham, NC 27708<br>(919)737-3067 |
| CAPSAS<br>Mark D. Shermis<br>EDB 504<br>The University of Texas<br>at Austin<br>Austin, TX 78712-1296<br>(512)471-4155 | HyperStat II<br>Mark D. Shermis<br>EDB 504<br>The University of Texas<br>at Austin<br>Austin, TX 787712-1296<br>(512)471-4155 | Statistical Consultant<br>National Collegiate<br>Software Clearinghouse<br>Duke University Press<br>6697 College Station<br>Durham, NC 27708<br>(919)737-3067 |
| | | Statistical Navigator<br>The Idea Works, Inc.<br>100 West Briarwood<br>Columbia, MO 65203<br>(800)537-4866 |

## META-ANALYSIS

At some point in the planning stages, the researcher must face the question of how much information must be obtained before a decision can be made. Gathering too much information wastes resources; gathering too little means the whole study goes to waste (Cohen, 1988). The "power" of a design is computed as a function of three variables: the anticipated effect size, the alpha level (Type I error rate) set by the researcher, and sample size. For example, the higher the effect size, the higher the alpha level, and the larger the sample, the more power a study has. While the researcher can fix *a priori* Type I error rates (e.g., rejecting a "true" null hypothesis), it is not possible to determine the power of a design until after the study is completed. To use the bridge example we introduced earlier, we can't determine how good the bridge is until after it is built. We can, however, estimate how good it should be before we build it.

One component of the planning process that can be estimated is the effect size of the independent variable. The technique used to estimate it is called meta-analysis. In meta-analysis, quantitative information from previous or pilot studies is combined to obtain an estimate of average effect size. This technique is useful for planning a replicated or related study or a meta-analysis study itself. Meta-analytic results generally are expressed in standard deviation units, or $\Delta$. A number of formulas are used to estimate an effect size. One formula designed to look at mean group differences is expressed as follows:

$$\Delta = \frac{\overline{X}_e - \overline{X}_c}{SD_p}$$

where
$\overline{X}_e$ represents the mean of the experimental group,
$\overline{X}_c$ represents the mean of the control group, and
$SD_p$ represents the pooled standard deviation of the two groups.*

Using our previous study example, let's say that a similar study conducted last year yielded an experimental problem-solving group mean of 12, a control group mean of 9, and a pooled standard deviation of 6. Using the formula above,

---

*Sometimes the standard deviation of the control group is used when the pooled standard deviation cannot be calculated.

$$\Delta = \frac{12 - 9}{6} = \frac{3}{6} = .5$$

That is, the performance of the experimental group was approximately half a standard deviation better than that of the control group.* Given a specified sample size, the $\Delta$ here represents the results of just one study. If we were to include results of other studies that used similar measures and different sample sizes, our estimates of $\Delta$ might vary. *Metastat*™, a subprogram of the statistical-analysis package *Pandora*™ (Veldman, 1989), is designed to help the researcher combine the results of various studies to estimate one average effect size. The program is helpful because it can evaluate $\Delta$ using a variety of inputs other than means and standard deviations. For example, some studies report only test statistics and degrees of freedom associated with the test, rather than individual means and standard deviations (e.g., *F* or *t*-values). Other studies report only the probability levels associated with the test statistics. *Metastat* can calculate $\Delta$ from sample information, test statistics, probability values, and correlations.

Suppose that you reviewed the research literature for innovative mathematical problem-solving approaches like the one illustrated earlier and discovered five studies directly related to the proposed intervention. The means, standard deviations, and *N*'s for each study are summarized in Table 4.2.

What kind of effect size would you estimate? With *Metastat*, a combined average effect of $\Delta$ can be calculated. The opening screen for the program consists of a menu of options available to the user, as displayed in Figure 4.9. For example, XTOP (pronounced "X to P") converts statistics to probabilities; COMPRO performs a meta-analysis of probabilities; XTOR ("X to R") converts statistics to correlations; RMETA performs a meta-analysis of correlations; EFFECT calculates effect size from sample statistics; DMETA performs a meta-analysis of effect sizes; and ANOVAN is an ANOVA analog with effect sizes or correlations. Notice that EFFECT has been chosen, a subprogram designed to calculate $\Delta$ from sample statistics.

Figure 4.10 illustrates the EFFECT input and output screen. We have taken the information from our first study (experimental group mean = 13, standard deviation = 8, *N* = 25; control group mean = 11, standard deviation = 10, *N* = 25) and entered it where requested. The program then calculated an effect size of .2174 (a small effect). In addition, EFFECT will calculate a variance estimate of $\Delta$, in this case

---

*Cohen (1988) characterizes studies with a $\Delta$ of .5 as having a "medium" impact.

TABLE 4.2.  Means, Standard Deviations, and N's of Five Hypothetical
            Problem-Solving Interventions.

| Study | Group | Mean | Standard Deviation | N |
|-------|-------|------|--------------------|---|
| 1 | E | 13 | 8 | 25 |
|   | C | 11 | 10 | 25 |
| 2 | E | 27 | 12 | 56 |
|   | C | 14 | 10 | 60 |
| 3 | E | 22 | 10 | 15 |
|   | C | 20 | 10 | 15 |
| 4 | E | 50 | 21 | 35 |
|   | C | 40 | 19 | 35 |
| 5 | E | 32 | 16 | 22 |
|   | C | 31 | 17 | 22 |

E = Experimental group, C = Control group

FIGURE 4.9.  Opening Screen of METASTAT module
             of *Pandora* (MS-DOS)

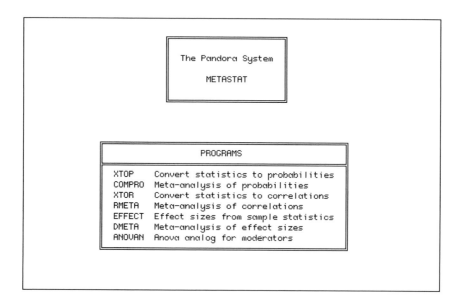

The Pandora System

METASTAT

PROGRAMS

| XTOP | Convert statistics to probabilities |
| COMPRO | Meta-analysis of probabilities |
| XTOR | Convert statistics to correlations |
| RMETA | Meta-analysis of correlations |
| EFFECT | Effect sizes from sample statistics |
| DMETA | Meta-analysis of effect sizes |
| ANOVAN | Anova analog for moderators |

.0805, along with $Z$ and $p$ values. We repeated this process for all five studies; the results are displayed in Table 4.3.

In Figure 4.11, we entered the individual effect sizes from the five problem-solving interventions into the DMETA procedure. Figure 4.12 shows the program's output file. A weighted average of $\Delta$, according to the information provided in the table, is about .58, which

FIGURE 4.10. METASTAT Module Supplying Means, Standard Deviations, and n's for the EFFECT procedure

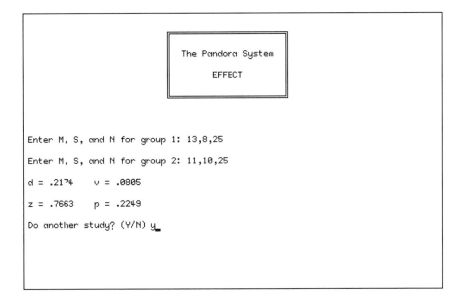

TABLE 4.3. Summary of Effect Sizes ($\Delta$) and Variances ($v$) for the Five Hypothetical Problem-Solving Interventions

| Study No. | $\Delta$ | $v$ |
|---|---|---|
| 1 | .2174 | .0805 |
| 2 | 1.1729 | .0405 |
| 3 | .1946 | .1340 |
| 4 | .4938 | .0589 |
| 5 | .0595 | .0909 |

## FIGURE 4.11. METASTAT Module Supplying Effect Sizes for the DMETA Procedure

```
                    ┌─────────────────────────┐
                    │  The Pandora System     │
                    │                         │
                    │        DMETA            │
                    └─────────────────────────┘


Enter d and v values:

Study 1 ? .2174,.0805

Study 2 ? 1.1729,.0405

Study 3 ? .1946,.134

Study 4 ? .4938,.0589

Study 5 ? .0595,.0909_
```

## FIGURE 4.12. METASTAT Module Output Showing Calculations for Estimating Overall Effect Size

```
OUT       PTF      314    2-12-90    9:53p
        18 File(s)     111616 bytes free

A:\>type out.ptf
Pandora system program DMETA

Meta-Analysis for Spelling Intervention

 .2174   .0805
1.1729   .0405
 .1946   .134
 .4938   .0589
 .0595   .0909


For the 5 studies:

Pooled d = .581
Pooled v = .0138
       z = 4.9486    p = 0

Homogeneity chi-square = 14.53
   with 4 df         p = .0061

A:\>_
```

## Meta-Analysis Software

| Apple Family | Apple Macintosh | IBM PC |
|---|---|---|
| | | META: Meta-Analysis Programs<br>National Collegiate Software Clearinghouse<br>Duke University Press<br>6697 College Station<br>Durham, NC 27708<br>(919)737-3067 |
| | | Pandora<br>Donald Veldman<br>EDB 504<br>The University of Texas at Austin<br>Austin, TX 78712-1296<br>(512)471-4155 |
| | | D Stat<br>Lawrence Erlbaum Assoc.<br>356 Broadway<br>Hillsdale, NJ 07642<br>(201)666-4110 |

would be characterized as a "medium" effect. That is, on the strength of information from the five studies selected for the meta-analysis, children participating in an intervention of the proposed type would, on average, be expected to perform better than controls by slightly more than one-half of a standard deviation.

Among other planning uses, the information obtained through meta-analysis can be used as input for calculations of sample size.

## STATISTICAL POWER ANALYSIS

The function of statistical power analysis is to help the researcher select a sample size sufficient to answer a question with a specified level of precision. One can also use the results of statistical power analysis to determine the probability of making a Type II error (failing to reject a false null hypothesis) for a given sample size. Programs of this type typically require four of five inputs: planned statistical analysis; estimated effect size; alpha level; anticipated beta level (for estimating sample size); and initial sample size (for power estimation). It should be clear by now that the steps of choosing appropriate statistics, calculating effect sizes, and determining sample size are interrelated activities. In this section we use *Statistical Power Analysis: A Computer Program*™ (Borenstein & Cohen, 1988) to demonstrate the steps of sample size/power estimation. The opening screen for the program is shown in Figure 4.13.

*Statistical Power Analysis: A Computer Program* is based primarily on the work by Cohen (1988). It assumes that any experimental design incorporates simple random assignment. Moreover, this PC/MS-DOS program makes calculations for only the most common planned statistical analyses and excludes a number of multivariate and nonparametric alternatives from its list of options. The basic core of the program is presented by a sequence of branching menu-driven choices.

In our previous example we calculated an average effect size of $\Delta = .58$ for the mathematical problem-solving intervention. Let's assume we were willing to bet that our proposed intervention was going to be at least as good as the "average" intervention of this type. In addition, let's further assume we planned on using an alpha level of .05 in performing an analysis of variance or covariance (depending on whether we use the *Test of Logical Thinking* scores as a covariate) to analyze our results. In Figure 4.14 we indicate to the program that we are planning a one-way analysis of variance, and in Figure 4.15 we ask the program to calculate statistical power.

FIGURE 4.13. Opening Screen of *Statistical Power Analysis* (MS-DOS)

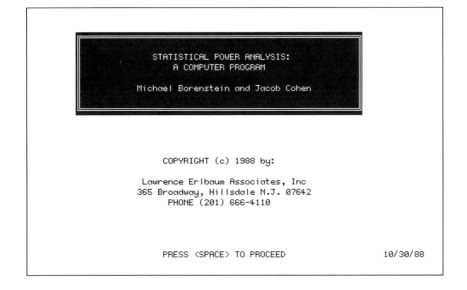

FIGURE 4.14.  Anticipated Statistical Analysis in *Statistical Power Analysis* Based on a One-Way Analysis of Variance

```
┌─────────────────────────────────────────────────┐
│    Cursor <UP> or <DOWN> -- Press Enter          │
├─────────────────────────────────────────────────┤
│      t-Test for Difference Between Means          │
│                 Correlation                       │
│          Arcsin Test for Proportions              │
│    Chi-Square for Proportions Without Yates       │
│     Chi-Square for Proportions With Yates         │
│███████████Oneway Analysis of Variance████████████│
│         Factorial Analysis of Variance            │
│             Multiple Regression                   │
│                 EXIT to DOS                       │
└─────────────────────────────────────────────────┘
```

FIGURE 4.15.  "Compute Power" Selection from *Statistical Power Analysis* (sample size and create graph/table of power are other options)

```
┌──────────────────────────────────────────┐
│   Cursor <UP> or <DOWN> -- Press Enter    │
├──────────────────────────────────────────┤
│███████████████Compute Power██████████████│
│        Create Tables/Graphs of Power      │
│            Exit from the Program          │
└──────────────────────────────────────────┘
```

In Figure 4.16, we are requested to provide the program with the estimated effect size (.580); an initial $N$ (20); the number of groups (2); and an alpha level (.050). The initial $N$ might be chosen from practical constraints or extrapolated from previous studies. Figure 4.17 illustrates the results of the first power analysis. Here, power is calculated as .706, a somewhat low value. If we were to base our design on this level of power, we essentially would be stipulating that Type II error is considered to be almost six times as serious as Type I error. Most researchers prefer a 4:1 ratio.

In Figure 4.18, we increase the $N$ to 24 while keeping the other program parameters constant. Figure 4.19 details the results of this change in terms of statistical power. Power has now increased to almost .80, bringing the beta-to-alpha ratio to about 4:1. We can now plan how large our sample should be. Allowing for a 10% attrition rate, we might plan to have a total $N$ of about 26 or 28. Some researchers like to have an even smaller beta-to-alpha ratio, but this obviously comes at the price of a larger sample size.

Not all types of research designs are addressed by the software mentioned above. For example, a research goal of many surveys may be to place a bound on the error of estimation (e.g., 3 percentage points) rather than to examine group differences. At the moment,

FIGURE 4.16. Entering Effect Size, Estimate of N, Number of Groups, and Alpha (*Statistical Power Analysis*)

```
         Cursor <UP><DOWN>   <LEFT><RIGHT> to Locate a Value
             Press <ESC> or <BACKSPACE> to Erase that Value
     Then use the TOP ROW of the keyboard to enter the new value
     <F9> PROCEED WITH COMPUTATIONS                     <F10> EXIT


   Effect Size f                      ▓ 0.580 ▓

   TOTAL N                                20
   Number of Groups                       2

   Alpha                               0.050




     Enter the Effect Size f,    or    <F1> General HELP Screen
     <F3> Enter Value for each cell    <F4> Enter Range of cells
     <F5> Enter Proportion Variance    <F6> View/Modify in Context
```

FIGURE 4.17.  Initial Power Estimate Based on Effect Size of .27, *N* of 60, and Two Groups (*Statistical Power Analysis*)

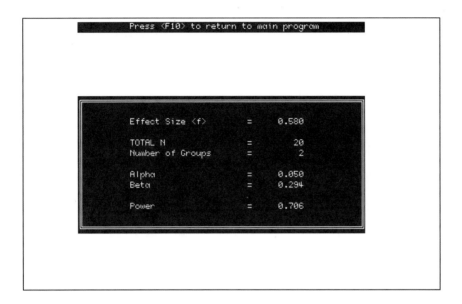

FIGURE 4.18.  Increasing *N* to Achieve an Acceptable Level of Power (*Statistical Power Analysis*)

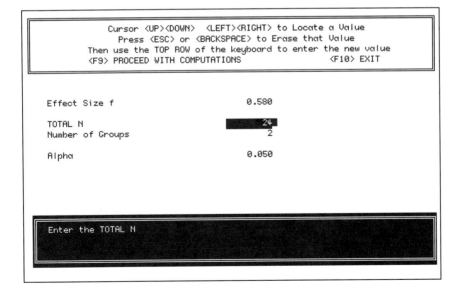

## FIGURE 4.19. Acceptable Level of Power Based on the New N (*Statistical Power Analysis*)

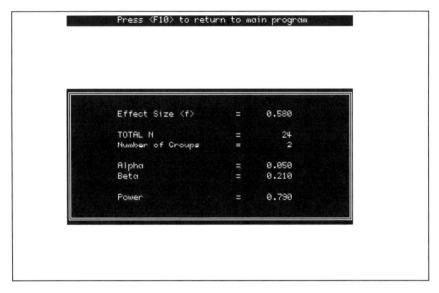

```
Press <F10> to return to main program


        Effect Size <f>       =      0.580

        TOTAL N               =        24
        Number of Groups      =         2

        Alpha                 =     0.050
        Beta                  =     0.210

        Power                 =     0.790
```

### Power/Sample Size Calculation Software

| Apple Family | Apple Macintosh | IBM PC |
| --- | --- | --- |
| Simple Sampling Plan Sourceview Software Intl. P.O. Box 578 Concord, CA 94522-0578 (415)686-8439 | Design Systat, Inc. 1800 Sherman Ave. Evanston, IL 60201 (708)864-5670 | Design Systat, Inc. 1800 Sherman Ave. Evanston, IL 60201 (708)864-5670 |
| Statistical Sample Planner Dynacomp, Inc. 178 Phillips Rd. Webster, NY 14580 (716)265-4040 | | Statistical Power Analysis Lawrence Erlbaum Associates, Inc. 365 Broadway Hillsdale, NJ 07642 (201)666-4110 |
| | | Stat Power Scientific Software, Inc. 1369 Neitzel Road Mooresville, IN 46158 (800)247-6113 |
| | | Ex-Sample+ The Idea Works, Inc. 100 West Briarwood Columbia, MO 65203 (800)537-4866 |

most statistical-power analysis software is geared toward experimental research, but we expect planning software for sampling-error estimation to be available soon.

## EXPERIMENTAL DESIGN SOFTWARE

If you happen to be using an experimental design, software that helps facilitate the design process is slowly becoming available. Most design software is geared toward studies that employ a repeated-measures data-collection strategy, a common approach in biomedical research and industrial applications. As with software which addresses the appropriate choice of statistical analysis, experimental-design software asks us the "right" questions, some of which we might not think of by ourselves. For example, the *Methodologist's Assistant*™, a subset of the *Methodologist's Toolchest*™ software by The Idea Works, Inc., provides a set of screens that ask about the goals of the research, data assumptions, and so on. Figure 4.20 shows the opening screen for this software. In addition, the *Methodologist's Toolchest* can provide assistance in questions dealing with statistical

FIGURE 4.20. Opening Screen of *Methodologist's Assistant*, Experimental Design Software (MS-DOS)

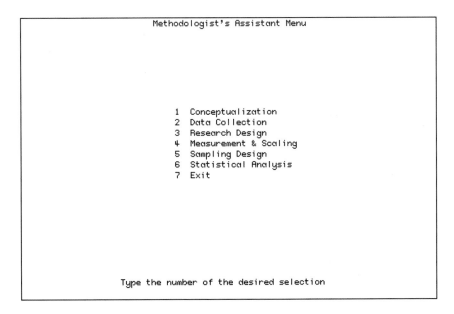

```
                        Methodologist's Assistant Menu




                    1  Conceptualization
                    2  Data Collection
                    3  Research Design
                    4  Measurement & Scaling
                    5  Sampling Design
                    6  Statistical Analysis
                    7  Exit




            Type the number of the desired selection
```

## Experimental Design Software

| Apple Family | Apple Macintosh | IBM PC |
|---|---|---|
| | | Designer Research Methodologist's Assistant The Idea Works, Inc. 100 West Briarwood Columbia, MO 65203 (800)537-4866 |
| | | ECHIP ECHIP, Inc. 7460 Lancaster Pike Hockessin, DE 19707 (302)239-5429 |
| | | DESIGN-EASE STAT-EASE, Inc. 4108 Aldrich Ave, So. Minneapolis, MN 55409 (612)822-5574 |

analysis, sampling design, measurement and scaling, and data collection.

## SUMMARY

Planning the operational aspects of your study can be a very tedious process. However, there is a growing field of software which can make this step easier and less demanding. The key to a successful design is, of course, asking the right questions (i.e., specifying the right questions). Microcomputer software, using artificial-intelligence techniques, can ask questions that will lead to the choice of an appropriate set of statistics. The software can lead you to think of alternatives or assumptions you normally might not consider. If you are contemplating an experimental or correlational design, meta-analysis software can help you estimate the anticipated effect of your intervention. This information is useful in estimating a reasonable sample size, another step that can be accomplished on the microcomputer. Finally, as we discuss in the next chapter, software is beginning to emerge that addresses the design of experiments and helps ensure greater efficiency of data collection.

# 5

# Data Collection

The microcomputer can be of enormous help to the researcher in the next step of the research cyle, data collection (Figure 5.1 and Table 5.1). By automating and streamlining this heretofore laborious process, the computer offers the researcher more freedom and greater accuracy and efficiency in data collection and measurement.

In conceptualizing how data might be collected, we have found it useful to distinguish between two types of microcomputer-enhanced techniques—*microcomputer-aided* data collection and *microcomputer-automated* data collection. Microcomputer-aided data collection requires intervention by the researcher/administrator in collecting the targeted information. Programs by which the researcher encodes observations into a microcomputer are an example. Microcomputer-automated data collection involves the collection of data directly by the microcomputer. Examples are devices that measure skin temperature, blood pressure, or galvanic skin response (GSR).

Actually, a third distinction could be made in our data-collection taxonomy: Microcomputer-assisted data collection involves entering data into a microcomputer through direct coding in real time, as in forms processing. We postpone this topic, however, until the next chapter, in which we discuss data management.

TABLE 5.1.    Research Matrix for Step 5 on the Research Cycle

| Research Task | Application | Use |
|---|---|---|
| **Step 5. Data Collection Strategies** | | |
| Write, organize, and field test instruments and procedures<br><br>Administer and supervise data collection | Computer-aided Survey Research, Forms-Processing, Observational Data-Collection Software, Analog-to-Digital Software/Hardware, Custom-developed Software, Courseware | Data collection may take a variety of forms. In conducting surveys, the researcher can use the microcomputer to design and administer the instrument. Surveys can be administered as self-completed instruments or over the phone via the computer-assisted telephone interview (CATI). In addition, forms processing can reduce or eliminate duplication of data entry.<br><br>Microcomputers also can be used to collect observational data. With appropriate software, laptop computers can enter a number of settings as nonintrusive "event recorders" for gathering valuable information.<br><br>In addition to aiding the data-collection process, microcomputers can automate it as well. Analog-to-digital information (e.g., temperature or sound data) can be picked up by the appropriate hardware/software combinations and written into a data file.<br><br>Finally, microcomputers can provide stimulus information. In one experiment, students are asked to estimate the position of an electronically simulated balloon. In the background, the position of the estimates, number of tries, and reaction times are all silently recorded. |

FIGURE 5.1. Data-Collection Strategies

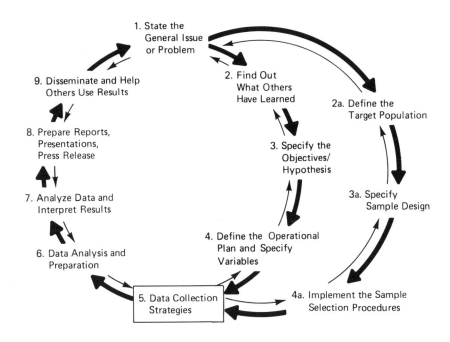

## MICROCOMPUTER-AIDED DATA COLLECTION

Microcomputer-aided data collection refers to the use of the computer in ancillary roles that might otherwise be performed by hand or by another device, such as a typewriter or event recorder. The first application we discuss is that of survey research, where microcomputers are used as a substitute for interview schedules, both in telephone interviewing and as an aid to face-to-face interviewing. We then illustrate the use of microcomputers as a tool for observation in field studies.

### Microcomputer-aided Survey Research

Perhaps the computer's greatest impact on survey methods has been in Computer-Assisted Telephone Interviewing (CATI). CATI utilizes a program that dials a respondent on a computer-administered interview schedule. Since CATI typically involves an interviewer, we consider it to be a type of computer-aided data collection. However, we know that now computers can administer questionnaires by harnessing text-to-speech conversion hardware and using the respondent's touch telephone as a means of response. Although the general public may not quite be ready for this type of survey, it does exemplify computer-automated research.

Computer administration of a survey has certain advantages over traditional forms of administration. The computer presents the question, error-checks the response, and verifies the answer. If an interviewer enters an incorrect response or "wild code"—a response outside the legitimate range of choices for that question—the computer indicates that an incorrect code has been given and asks for a new one. Most CATI programs also allow entry of open-ended questions, but utilize no error-checking procedure for this type of question (other than perhaps spellchecking).

Once a response is verified by the interviewer, the CATI program automatically branches to the next appropriate question. The ability to dynamically branch is important because in a complicated survey, interviewers might solicit information that is inapplicable to the respondent. For example, Question 1 of a survey might ask the respondent to indicate whether he or she is single, married, divorced, or widowed, and questions Questions 2–5 might pertain only to married respondents. In the CATI environment, if a respondent answered "single," "divorced," or "widowed" to Question 1, Questions 2–5 would be skipped automatically and Question 6 would be presented to the interviewer as the next query. This eliminates one potential source of coding error.

Data encoded by CATI can be stored on either a floppy or hard disk to be analyzed later. Of course, responses to open-ended questions will require some type of additional coding before being saved in a form that is suitable for data analysis.

*Q-Fast*™, from StatSoft Software, Inc., incorporates many of the features mentioned above. It includes: (1) a procedure to generate a script of an interview for later recall and presentation, (2) a subroutine that writes the results of the survey in a format that can be read by a data-analysis program, and (3) a subprogram which gives a simple display of the results of data gathering. *Q-Fast* does not incorporate any algorithms for telephone dialing or call-status monitoring.

The opening screen from *Q-Fast* shown in Figure 5.2 lists the program's options. In Figure 5.3, the program asks a hypothetical question about whether or not the respondent has taken a vacation. If the respondent were to answer "yes" to one of the first two options, the program would ask a series of follow-up questions on how he or she spent the vacation. If the respondent were to answer "no," the program

FIGURE 5.2.   Opening Screen from *Q-Fast*, a Microcomputerized
Questionnaire Administration System (MS-DOS)

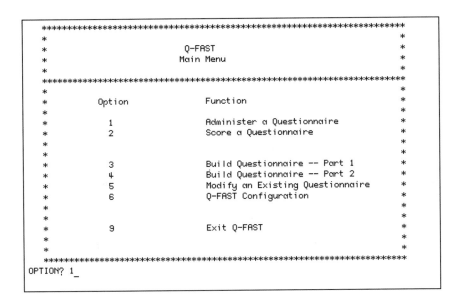

```
*******************************************************************
*                                                                 *
*                         Q-FAST                                  *
*                       Main Menu                                *
*                                                                 *
*******************************************************************
*                                                                 *
*        Option                  Function                        *
*                                                                 *
*          1                  Administer a Questionnaire         *
*          2                  Score a Questionnaire             *
*                                                                 *
*                                                                 *
*          3                  Build Questionnaire -- Part 1     *
*          4                  Build Questionnaire -- Part 2     *
*          5                  Modify an Existing Questionnaire  *
*          6                  Q-FAST Configuration              *
*                                                                 *
*                                                                 *
*          9                  Exit Q-FAST                       *
*                                                                 *
*                                                                 *
*******************************************************************
OPTION? 1_
```

FIGURE 5.3.   A Question Administered by *Q-Fast*

```
# 4
Have you taken a vacation in the past six months?

1 Yes - Four days or more
2 Yes - Less than four days
3 No

What is your choice ==> 3
```

would branch to the next applicable question. *Q-Fast* is available for both MS-DOS and Macintosh microcomputers.

### Face-to-Face Interviews

Groves and Kahn (1979) note that approximately eight percent of the U.S. population is without access to a home telephone. This figure is deceptive, since it includes individuals who are temporarily without telephones because they are in the process of moving. To correct the coverage bias associated with non-ownership of a telephone, a number of authors have advocated the use of a dual sampling frame—one for a telephone sample and a supplementary frame for face-to-face interviews. Theoretically, information gathered from the face-to-face interview (which has a higher coverage rate) could be used to correct for bias occasioned by non-ownership of a telephone in the larger sample.

Computers can aid in the process of gathering information by face-to-face interview. For example, the data-collector can use a small, battery-powered microcomputer to administer the survey in the respondent's home. The interviewer would have the same full error-checking and keyboard-entry capabilities as a telephone interviewer. Additionally, the interviewer could administer graphic representations of rating scales, ladders, thermometers, etc., to the respondent, eliminating the need to describe such devices verbally. (These would be the equivalent of "show cards," which are common in face-to-face surveys.) Furthermore, the respondent could read along with the interviewer as questions were presented. The interviewer would be available to motivate and probe, but the task of providing responses could be made more interesting. Figure 5.4 shows an example of a response format composed with *Inquire*™, an interviewing software package which runs on MS-DOS-compatible machines.

### Self-Completed Mail Questionnaires

This section discusses potential applications of the microcomputer to self-completed questionnaires. Conjecture about applications here is somewhat problematic, for while microcomputers have become very popular, there are still many homes which do not yet have them. Even more troublesome to the questionnaire administrator is the diversity of machines for those individuals who do own

FIGURE 5.4. Editing an Open-Ended Questionnaire Item
on Inquire (MS-DOS)

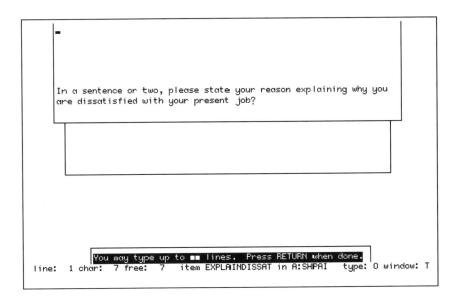

them. Nevertheless, four scenarios for self-administered question-naires have either been used or envisioned:

1. The survey is administered in one central location (e.g., a hospital ward), and respondents complete the question-naire when their schedules permit, but within a prescribed time. For example, because of nurses' diverse schedules, it is difficult to assemble all of them at one time for the admin-istration of a questionnaire. However, if the questionnaire were administered via a microcomputer left at the nurses' station, nurses could complete the survey when they had a few minutes free during their shift.

2. The survey administrator puts the questionnaire on a mi-crocomputer and respondents self-administer the question-naire from a remote terminal. The program could provide error-checking routines, verification, and graphic displays as an enhancement to most common formats.

3. Respondents are sent a diskette and asked to run the survey program on their own machines, similar to the procedure for completing a mail questionnaire. After completing the

questionnaire, the respondent returns the floppy disk so that the data can be entered into another computer for analysis, or the data are sent by a telecommunications modem from one computer to another. This approach is quite useful in government, business, or education, where specific forms and machine formats are common (although prescreening to ensure compatibility with the study's software may be required). A number of marketing firms have used this approach successfully by providing the respondent an incentive (e.g., a free video game or diskette) in return for completing the survey.

4. Using "electronic mail," a researcher administers the questionnaire via a computer network (e.g., CompuServe). Such networks usually permit the sending of messages back and

## Survey Research Software

| Apple Family | Apple Macintosh | IBM PC |
|---|---|---|
| Q-Fast<br>StatSoft, Inc.<br>2832 East 10th St., Ste. 4<br>Tulsa, OK 74104<br>(918)583-4149 | Q-Fast<br>StatSoft, Inc.<br>2832 East 10th St., Ste. 4<br>Tulsa, OK 74104<br>(918)583-4149 | Q-Fast<br>StatSoft, Inc.<br>2832 East 10th St., Ste. 4<br>Tulsa, OK 74104<br>(918)583-4149 |
| Teleofacts<br>Teleofacts 2<br>Dilithium Press Software<br>P.O. Box 606<br>Beaverton, OR 97075<br>(503)243-3313 | MacCATI<br>PSRC Software<br>302 Hayes Hall<br>Bowling Green, OH 43403<br>(419)372-8648 | Inquire<br>New Era Software<br>P.O. Box 615<br>North Amherst, MA 01059 |
| Telephone Survey<br>Persimmon Software<br>1901 Gemway Dr.<br>Charlotte, NC 28216<br>(704)398-1309 | MacInterview Release 1.7<br>Erich Breitschwerdt and<br>Partner<br>Paulsmuhlenstrasse 41<br>4000 Dusseldorf 13<br>West Germany<br>0211-7182232 | Measurement & Scaling<br>Strategist<br>The Idea Works, Inc.<br>100 West Briarwood<br>Columbia, MO 65203<br>(800)537-4866 |
| Surveyworks<br>K-12 Micro Media Publishing<br>6 Arrow Rd.<br>Ramsey, NJ 07466<br>(201)825-8888 | | Survey I<br>National Collegiate<br>Software Clearinghouse<br>Duke University Press<br>6697 College Station<br>Durham, NC 27708<br>(919)737-3067 |

forth to individuals across the nation (e.g., "Would you be willing to participate in a study of. . . ?"). Respondents who choose to participate access a file on the network and self-administer the questionnaire, and the study director retrieves the data later. (Of course, the researcher should be mindful of the fact that such audiences represent a somewhat narrow population of persons heavily involved in computers and telecommunications.)

While surveys represent a mode of data collection that has increased in popularity in recent years, they are by no means the only technique of data collection that has been aided by the computer.

### Forms Processing

In forms processing, the collected information generally is static and is the same for all respondents. An example is a biographical survey or application blank with questions a company uniformly asks all respondents. The data can be entered into the computer directly by the respondent, by a secretary transcribing the respondent's written information, or by a data collector as he or she interviews the respondent next to the computer. One useful feature of the current generation of electronic forms is that they can be made to look like their paper-and-pencil counterparts. Many institutions find it cost effective to present information in both media. For example, a number of colleges are now waiving application fees if the candidate will file an electronic form rather than the paper-and-pencil version. This reduces the college's data-processing costs and speeds up the processing of applications. Figure 5.5 illustrates an electronic form generated by the database program *Filemaker® II*.

### Observation Tools

The major tools for systematically recording observations are paper-and-pencil-based instruments. However, paper-and-pencil methods are far from the perfect solution. The sheer size, weight, and volume of paper limits the number of variables and observations that can be obtained. Observing more than one behavior or subject adds to the difficulty and complexity of the task. In addition, paper-and-pencil-recorded data typically are "reduced" and analyzed by a calculator or computer, and the process of transferring data from paper

FIGURE 5.5.  An Example of Forms Processing on *FileMaker II*
(Macintosh)

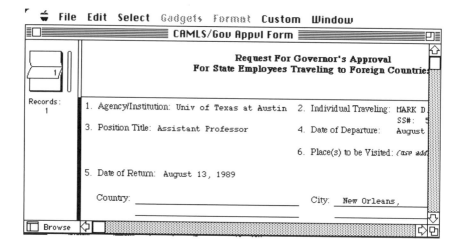

## Forms Processing Software

| Apple Family | Apple Macintosh | IBM PC |
|---|---|---|
| Forms Foundry<br>American Eagle Software,<br>Inc.<br>P.O. Box 46080<br>Lincolnwood, IL 60646<br>(312)792-1227 | Smartform<br>Claris Corp.<br>5201 Patrick Henry Dr.<br>P.O. Box 58168<br>Santa Clara, CA 95052<br>(800)544-8554 | Quickform<br>United Systems Software<br>Corporation<br>955 East Javelina Ave.<br>Suite 200<br>Mesa, AZ 85204<br>(602)892-7974 |
| | Fast Forms<br>Power Up Software Corp.<br>2929 Campus Drive<br>San Mateo, CA 94403<br>(800)851-2917<br>(800)223-1479 in CA | Formsfile<br>Power Up Software Corp.<br>2929 Campus Drive<br>San Mateo, CA 94403<br>(800)851-2917<br>(800)223-1479 in CA |
| | Trueform<br>Adobe Systems Inc.<br>1585 Charleston Road<br>P.O. Box 7900<br>Mountain View, CA<br>94039-7900<br>(800)344-8335 | Formworx<br>Formworx Corp.<br>1601 Trapelo Rd.<br>Reservoir Pl.<br>Waltham, MA 02154<br>(617)890-4499 |

to an electronic device is not only laborious but provides numerous opportunities for error.

The speed and accuracy of a calculator or digital computer usually outweigh its expense.* Specific mechanical and electronic devices have been configured for data collection and analysis. More recently, microcomputer programs have been written to perform these counting functions.

### Mechanical and Other Tallying Methods

If an observer is interested in recording behaviors, there are several alternatives to paper-and-pencil tallying. One researcher's strategy was to empty her pocket of all coins, place a coin into her pocket each time the target behavior occurred, and simply count the number of coins at the end of the session. This technique works fine, but if the frequency of the target behavior requires a great number of coins, it can be rather hard on one's pocket!

Another convenient method is to use a click counter, a small, hand-held device about the size of a large keychain. When a button on the side of the counter is pressed, the internal digital counter increases by one. These types of counters typically are used by golfers to keep track of their strokes or by department stores to keep track of the number of customers entering the store.

More recently, small pocket calculators have been used. The observer simply carries the calculator and presses a key to add one number to the memory. If the calculator has several memory keys, then multiple behaviors or multiple subjects can be recorded. With a printing calculator, the numbers representing behaviors can be printed on the paper tape as they happen and tallied afterwards (Edelson, 1978).

### Hand-Held Event Recorders

Small, hand-held, battery-powered data-collection (and sometimes analysis) devices are a definite aid to the observer. They require little formal training to operate. The operator presses a num-

---

*Data that is input into a computer usually goes through a process of (1) coding, (2) entry into a computer via a terminal or data cards, (3) verification and wild code checking.

ber key that represents the behavior being recorded. Results of the observation usually can be defined by sequences, frequencies, and durations, which are stored in memory and later recalled for analysis. Because of their ease of use, they are faster and more accurate than paper-and-pencil methods. These devices are commonly found in educational, business, and industrial settings.

Depending on what the device is required to do (and your own mechanical ability), small portable devices can be "homemade" (cf. Baker & Whitehead, 1972). On the other hand, very sophisticated data-collection/analysis devices such as the Datamyte 800™ series* are available.

## Event Recording with Microcomputers

The microcomputer can be programmed to function just like an event-recording device. In this section we discuss a sample program using an MS-DOS microcomputer. Researchers typically use a program like this on a small laptop computer, the smallest of which is the about the size of a VHS cassette tape.

The computer program is called the Behavioral Event Recording Package (*BERP*™).[†] *BERP* is a multichannel, simultaneous behavioral-event recorder. It records up to ten events,[‡] storing the sequence of behaviors, the onset (beginning) time, and the cessation (ending) time. The data are stored on a floppy disk and can be printed on a printer. *BERP* runs in three computer formats—MS-DOS, Macintosh, and Apple II.

Let's look at an example to see how *BERP* operates. Figure 5.6 illustrates the opening screen for the program. The key definitions are created in a separate program and are configured by the researcher. In one study the "A" could refer to the number of shoppers stopping by a display; in another study the same key could refer to the attention span of a child performing some problem-solving task.

Pressing any of the defined keys causes the computer to record the sequence and onset of the behavior defined by that key, as is illustrated in Figure 5.7. Pressing the key a second time will record the

---

*Datamyte is the trademark of Electro/General Corporation, Minnetoka, Minnesota.

[†]Developed by Paul Stemmer, Ph.D., at the University of Michigan, School of Education.

[‡]The program can be modified to handle more than ten events. The ten events correspond to the ten digits on the human hand.

FIGURE 5.6.  Opening Screen for the *Behavioral Event Recorder Package (BERP)* (MS-DOS)

```
            THE UNIVERSITY OF MICHIGAN SCHOOL OF EDUCATION

                    E V E N T   R E C O R D E R


PRESS <A>...<T> FOR EVENT, <Y> FOR PAUSE, AND <Z> FOR PAUSE END

PRESS <X> WHEN FINISHED WITH EVENT


A problem-solving   B int_w_subjects   C int_w_experimenterD distracted
E review_mats       F review_choice    G                   H
I                   J                  K                   L
M                   N                  O                   P
Q                   R                  S                   T

............................................................
```

FIGURE 5.7.  Choosing Event "A" — Problem-Solving in *BERP*

```
            THE UNIVERSITY OF MICHIGAN SCHOOL OF EDUCATION

                    E V E N T   R E C O R D E R


PRESS <A>...<T> FOR EVENT, <Y> FOR PAUSE, AND <Z> FOR PAUSE END

PRESS <X> WHEN FINISHED WITH EVENT


A problem-solving   B int_w_subjects   C int_w_experimenterD distracted
E review_mats       F review_choice    G                   H
I                   J                  K                   L
M                   N                  O                   P
Q                   R                  S                   T

...▣.......................▣.......................
```

## Observational Research Software

| Apple Family | Apple Macintosh | IBM PC |
|---|---|---|
| BERP<br>Carl F. Berger<br>School of Education<br>University of Michigan<br>Ann Arbor, MI 48109<br>(313)763-4678 | BERP<br>Carl F. Berger<br>School of Education<br>University of Michigan<br>Ann Arbor, MI 48109<br>(313)763-4678 | BERP<br>Carl F. Berger<br>School of Education<br>University of Michigan<br>Ann Arbor, MI 48109<br>(313)763-4678 |
|  | Observer Software<br>Richard Deni<br>32 Merritt Dr.<br>Lawrenceville, NJ 08648 | Eventlog<br>Conduit<br>University of Iowa<br>Oakdale Campus<br>Iowa City, IA 52242<br>(319)335-4100 |

cessation time. It should be noted that the program can track all ten (or more) behaviors simultaneously. At the end of the observation session, the "Q" key is pressed, which ends the program and records the session. The data are recorded automatically on floppy disk for later retrieval.

By recording the data in electronic form, the possibility of human error in the transfer process is eliminated. Moreover, the microcomputer has made performance of this very complex task a little easier, and fewer demands on the observers should make for more reliable coding of behaviors. Once observers know which keys to press, they need not take their eyes off the subjects, as they would if they were writing down their observations.

Hand-held recorders and the microcomputer are observation instruments in the true sense of the word. They are tools of the trade which not only make the task easier, but the results more accurate. Moreover, data can be transferred from these devices via computer network to mini- and mainframe computers for complex time-series analysis.

## MICROCOMPUTER-AUTOMATED DATA COLLECTION

In microcomputer-automated data collection, the computer is directed to perform all the steps of data acquisition—it provides the stimuli and collects, codes, and stores responses automatically.

Two examples of microcomputer-automated observation are illustrated in this section. In the first example, we show how data can be collected for science experiments with analog-to-digital conversion techniques. "Analog-to-digital conversion" is the process of collecting data (e.g., temperature) by analog devices, then converting the data to digital form, which subsequently can be processed by a computer. In the second example, we follow through with our hypothetical study on problem-solving strategies by demonstrating a game program called *DARTS*. The game consists of an animated simulation of a dart being thrown at a balloon. The objective of the game is to estimate what coordinates would cause the dart to hit and pop the balloon. During the simulation, the number of trials, the subject's accuracy in guessing the coordinates, and the subject's reaction time are observed, counted, and recorded by the microcomputer. The researcher can make relevant qualitative observations, free from the burden of quantitative data recording.

### Analog-to-Digital Devices

One example of analog-to-digital conversion is the digital thermostat. The temperature-sensing apparatus of the thermostat is the analog part of the device. Once the thermostat performs its monitoring function, the analog signals must be converted to digital form for processing by a microcomputer on a chip. After processing, the information is re-converted to analog form as voltage, which controls the heating/cooling mechanism (Shermis & Givner, 1986).

There are three types of basic signals used in analog-to-digital conversion:

1. The basic analog signal can take on any value in either range or domain. For example, with a programmable thermostat, the domain could be labeled in units of time, with zero being the turn-on point (Carr, 1980).

2. A sampled signal is an analog signal which is allowed to exist for only instants in time. There are rules regarding the rate at which signals are sampled. For example, the Nyquist Rule stipulates that the sampling must be set at least twice the highest frequency component present in the waveform being sampled. That is, a periodic signal with a basic frequency of about 3 Hz (e.g., the arterial-blood-pressure waveform of someone exercising), which could be sampled up to

the fifth harmonic, would have to be sampled at least 36 times per second (Wyss, 1984).

3. A digital signal is a variation of a sampled signal. A digital signal usually is produced by a sample-and-hold (S&H) circuit. Typically, a switch is closed to admit the signal and then re-opened after the signal is measured. In most cases, the instantaneous value of the signal is stored in a capacitor (Carr, 1980).

Shermis and Givner (1986) document a number of ways that analog-to-digital conversion can facilitate research in working with children who have special disabilities. Input devices include light pens, graphics tablets, joysticks, keypads, and microphones. Data can be taken on levels of motoric activity, response time and accuracy, sound level and production, light, temperature, and pressure.

Figure 5.8 shows light information being displayed from the SADC 8000, an analog-to-digital board manufactured by Berger Industries. The SADC 8000, which works with almost any board with an RS-232 serial port, takes analog information and converts it to digital form for processing by a computer. Figure 5.8 illustrates the version of the software displayed on the Macintosh computer. It shows a constant light level which drops after a period of time. Figure 5.9 il-

FIGURE 5.8. Measurement of Light by the *SADC 8000* (Macintosh)

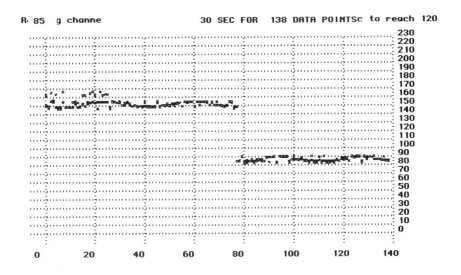

lustrates fluctuations in temperature with the same analog-to-digital board, but with a different input device—a thermistor. A social or clinical psychologist might use such information to determine whether a discussion was becoming anxiety provoking for a subject. The software can also store information in a data file for subsequent analysis.

FIGURE 5.9. Measurement of Temperature by the *SADC 8000*

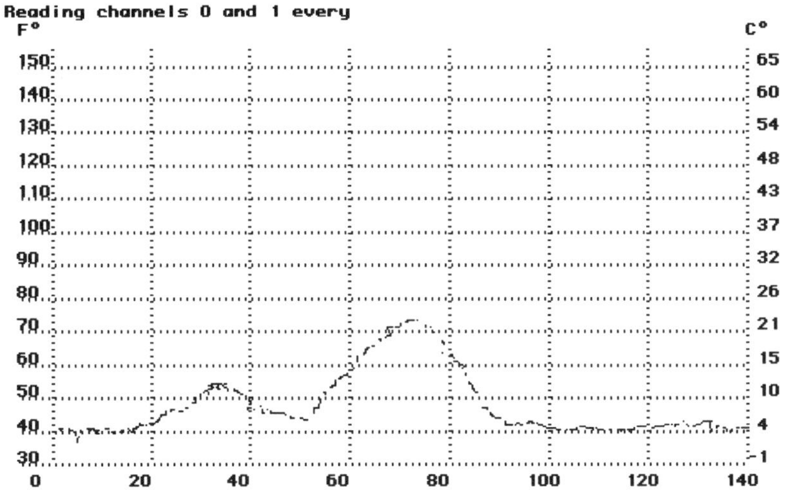

Specialized Data-Collection Software or Courseware

The computer also can be used to generate stimuli and record the responses of subjects. One example of this technique is illustrated by the program *DARTS*. This program is an adaptation of the *DARTS* simulation on the PLATO™ time-sharing computer system. The program has been adapted for almost all of the popular microcomputers and can provide an excellent tool for discovering how students approach and make progress on tasks involving mathematical skill.*

*Listings for the *DARTS* programs are available from Dr. Carl F. Berger, School of Education, University of Michigan, Ann Arbor, MI 48109.

### Analog-to-Digital Software/Hardware

| Apple Family | Apple Macintosh | IBM PC |
|---|---|---|
| SADC 8000<br>Berger Industries<br>605 Reid Rd., Ste. 10<br>Grand Blanc, MI 48434 | SADC 8000<br>Berger Industries<br>605 Reid Rd., Ste. 10<br>Grand Blanc, MI 48434 | SADC 8000<br>Berger Industries<br>605 Reid Rd., Ste. 10<br>Grand Blanc, MI 48434 |
| Adalab<br>Interactive Microware, Inc.<br>P.O. Box 139<br>State College, PA 16804<br>(800)832-3021 | BenchTop<br>Metaresearch, Inc.<br>516 SE Morrison, Ste. M-1<br>Portland, OR 97214<br>(503)238-5728 | Adalab<br>Quick I/O<br>Labtech Notebook<br>Interactive Microware, Inc.<br>P.O. Box 139<br>State College, PA 16804<br>(800)832-3021 |
| Analog Connection<br>Strawberry Tree, Inc.<br>160 S. Wolfe Rd.<br>Sunnyvale, CA 94086<br>(408)736-8800 | The ADC-1 Data<br>Acquisition and Control<br>System<br>Remote Measurement<br>Systems, Inc.<br>2633 Eastlake Ave. East<br>Suite 200<br>Seattle, WA 98102<br>(206)328-2255 | Analog Connection<br>Strawberry Tree, Inc.<br>160 S. Wolfe Rd.<br>Sunnyvale, CA 94086<br>(408)736-8800 |
| Collection<br>Persimmon Software<br>1901 Gemway Dr.<br>Charlotte, NC 28216<br>(704)398-1309 | MacLab<br>World Precision<br>Instruments, Inc.<br>375 Quinnipiac Ave.<br>New Haven, CT 06513<br>(203)469-8281 | |

*DARTS* begins by asking the student for a student identification number, age, and grade in school. After the researcher explains the procedure to the student, the simulation begins. Figures 5.10 through 5.12 illustrate how the simulation might look to the subject. In Figure 5.10, a balloon has appeared. In Figure 5.11, the subject has estimated where on the "wall" the balloon lies and fired a dart. In Figure 5.12, we see that the subject correctly estimated the position of the balloon—the dart has popped it. By using the computer to capture all the quantitative information, the researcher is free to record anecdotal or other qualitative information.

Newman and Berger (1984) used the *DARTS* program to collect data on number-estimation strategies used by middle-school children. Their analysis led the authors to conclude that children used three prevailing strategies:

1. a "straddling" approach, where the subject overestimates and underestimates the target before hitting it;
2. a "successive approximations" approach, where estimates from one direction (either over or under) hit closer to the target;
3. random guessing.

FIGURE 5.10. A Balloon Appearing on the Wall in the DARTS Simulation

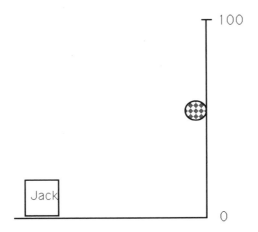

FIGURE 5.11. A Dart is Released Towards the Balloon

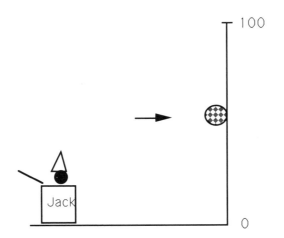

FIGURE 5.12. An Accurate Estimate Results in a "Popped" Balloon

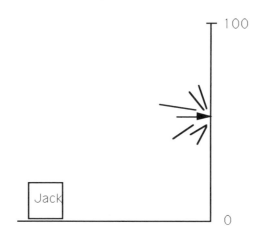

A child using a particular strategy might benefit from a tailored instructional intervention which capitalized on the strengths (or weaknesses) associated with that strategy. In more recent work, this study was extended to children's estimation of logarithmic scales (Berger, Pintrich, & Stemmer, 1987).

### Automated Data-Collection Programs

| Apple Family | Apple Macintosh | IBM PC |
|---|---|---|
| Computer Lab in Memory and Cognition Conduit University of Iowa Oakdale Campus Iowa City, IA 52242 (319)335-4100 | MacLab for Psychology (I & II) Intellimation 130 Cremona Dr. P.O. Box 1922 Santa Barbara, CA 93116-1922 (800)346-8355 | MemLab National Collegiate Software Clearinghouse Duke University Press 6697 College Station Durham, NC 27708 (919)737-3067 |
| Psych Lab HRM Software/Div. of Queue 562 Boston Ave. Bridgeport, CT 06610 (203)335-0906 | MindLab Blake Meike Kiewiet Computation Center Dartmouth College Hanover, NH 03755 (603)646-2643 | |

## SUMMARY

This chapter has dealt with some of the various ways a microcomputer is used to gather and transfer data before analysis. We expect to see the popularity of computerized data-collection strategies increase significantly in the near future. In addition to improving accuracy and efficiency, the researcher bypasses a number of laborious steps, since the data are rendered almost directly into electronic digital form, ready for analysis. In the next chapter we discuss managing data and using the microcomputer for data analysis.

# 6

# Analyzing Results

## INTRODUCTION

Using a computer of any kind to conduct a data analysis is an obvious and accepted practice. Researchers who have been using mainframe and minicomputers for data analysis may be very comfortable with these processes. Why should they change? In this chapter we examine microcomputer packages that help the researcher analyze quantitative (and qualitative) data. While we mention a variety of statistical-analysis packages, we highlight *Systat*® from Systat, Inc., for four important reasons. First, *Systat* is one of the most comprehensive microcomputer packages available. Its capabilities rival those of many mainframe computer packages. Second, *Systat* operates on a variety of hardware systems, including MS-DOS, Macintosh, NCR Tower (UNIX), and VAX (CMS). Third, *Systat* is relatively easy to run and uses simple command instructions from line-oriented operating systems, or menu selections from graphics-oriented environments. Finally, *Systat* is flexible and can be applied in a number of unique analytic situations.

In the first section of this chapter we describe various aspects of managing and storing data. In the second section we discuss the advantages and disadvantages of using a microcomputer for data analysis. Figure 6.1 and Table 6.1 illustrate these steps as part of the research cycle.

FIGURE 6.1. Issues in Data Preparation and Analysis

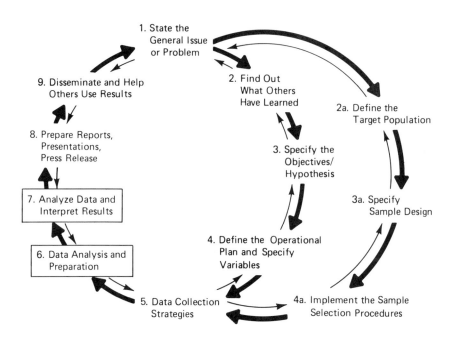

## DATA PREPARATION AND STORAGE

Each data-gathering scheme described thus far essentially has consisted of ways to enter data into a text or data file. In this section we discuss methods of data input, preparing data for analysis, data archiving, and data analysis.

### Types of Data Input

There are four general strategies for transcribing data collected by an instrument (e.g., a self-completed mail questionnaire) into a computer file that can be stored for later retrieval. These strategies include direct data entry, the use of punched or marked cards, optical character recognition, and keying the data. So far, only one of the methods—direct data entry—has been described thoroughly, but the other three methods may be just as helpful in this aspect of your study.

Table 6.1.  Research Matrix for Steps 6 and 7 on the Research Cycle

| Research Task | Application | Use |
|---|---|---|
| **Step 6. Data Analysis Preparation** | | |
| Prepare Data for Analysis | Scanning Software/ Hardware; Word Processing, Database Management, and Statistical Analysis Software | Data may be entered through a number of mechanisms, including direct data entry, punched or marked cards, optical character recognition, and keying. Because errors may be introduced during this process, it is important to check the quality of data once entered. |
| **Step 7. Data Analysis** | | |
| Analyze Data and Interpret Results | Statistical-Analysis Software, Spreadsheets, and Graphics Software | Microcomputers can be used to visualize data in order to understand their structure and distribution. Descriptive and inferential statistics can be generated to make conclusions about the study's results. With respect to inferential statistics, both parametric and nonparametric tools are available to the researcher. Finally, not all data can be analyzed by strictly quantitative techniques. Qualitative data (e.g., text) can be abstracted effectively as well. |

*Direct Data Entry*   Direct data entry is a technique whereby the computer gathers information directly and writes the data to a computer text file. The DARTS program mentioned in Chapter 5 typifies such a program in that it records students' estimations, time latency, student numbers, and additional background information. The researcher need not handle the data at all, but can later access and analyze the resultant computer file. The forms-processing software mentioned in Chapter 5 also illustrates this direct data entry; information entered into the form fields is written to a computer data file such as the one shown in Figure 6.2.

The advantages of direct data entry are many: (1) Data are collected by a real-time mechanism and do not have to be entered "after the fact"; (2) the computer can check wild codes automatically; (3) the computer normally provides immediate feedback if improper/inapplicable data are collected; (4) this method generally leads to fewer steps in data analysis; and (5) cost savings usually result.

FIGURE 6.2. Example of a "Flat File" Created with
Forms-Processing Software

| ID# | AG | GR | SX | IQ | RDG | ART | DX | CLEI | SRS | PRF | SRS | RAW |
|---|---|---|---|---|---|---|---|---|---|---|---|---|
| 85046 | 6 | 6 | 1 | 108 | 123 | 130 | E | 5 | OP | 98 | 60 | 59 |
| 85050 | 8 | 3 | 1 | 103 | 118 | 94 | E | 7 | PR | 102 | 64 | 58 |
| 85062 | 9 | 3 | 1 | 118 | 90 | 120 | L | 5 | RZ | 72 | 52 | 49 |
| 85071 | 10 | 5 | 1 | 103 | 94 | 107 | E | 11 | PA | 101 | 63 | 65 |
| 85075 | 11 | 5 | 1 | 93 | 98 | 94 | E | 6 | RA | 103 | 64 | 61 |
| 85077 | 13 | 7 | 1 | 102 | 87 | 101 | E | 5 | ZZ | 71 | 48 | 52 |
| 85083 | 10 | 5 | 0 | 126 | 112 | 109 | E | 8 | AP | 96 | 67 | 74 |
| 85099 | 9 | 4 | 1 | 112 | 111 | 108 | E | 16 | AP | 106 | 65 | 65 |
| 85108 | 11 | 5 | 1 | 84 | 89 | 74 | E | 8 | RP | 104 | 65 | 58 |
| 85109 | 7 | 1 | 1 | 100 | 84 | 83 | E | 3 | ZZ | 62 | 48 | 51 |
| 85119 | 9 | 4 | 0 | 111 | 109 | 117 | E | 6 | OA | 75 | 58 | 62 |
| 85122 | 12 | 6 | 1 | 110 | 96 | 81 | E | 19 | ZZ | 74 | 53 | 44 |
| 85124 | 13 | 8 | 1 | 94 | 108 | 103 | E | 10 | ZZ | 85 | 53 | 50 |
| 85126 | 13 | 8 | 0 | 121 | 116 | 112 | N | 4 | ZZ | 61 | 48 | 51 |
| 85127 | 8 | 2 | 1 | 94 | 80 | 77 | L | 11 | ZZ | 73 | 52 | 50 |
| 85129 | 6 | 1 | 1 | 99 | 100 | 97 | L | 8 | ZZ | 71 | 49 | 47 |
| 86003 | 9 | 4 | 1 | 103 | 103 | 105 | E | 14 | RP | 97 | 62 | 52 |
| 86006 | 14 | 9 | 1 | 86 | 99 | 87 | E | 7 | PZ | 94 | 57 | 53 |
| 86012 | 13 | 7 | 1 | 92 | 119 | 89 | E | 14 | PA | 119 | 66 | 64 |
| 86015 | 10 | 4 | 0 | 95 | 88 | 86 | E | 14 | PZ | 88 | 64 | 58 |
| 86018 | 8 | 2 | 1 | 97 | 86 | 77 | E | 15 | OZ | 80 | 55 | 55 |
| 86020 | 9 | 4 | 1 | 127 | 116 | 105 | E | 10 | RD | 112 | 68 | 64 |
| 86021 | 9 | 4 | 1 | 109 | 92 | 116 | E | 16 | AP | 90 | 59 | 62 |
| 86024 | 6 | 1 | 0 | 96 | 108 | 118 | E | 5 | OZ | 54 | 54 | 59 |
| 86026 | 8 | 2 | 0 | 122 | 107 | 110 | E | 7 | ZZ | 57 | 51 | 52 |

**Page 1**                     **Normal+...**

As with most aspects of conducting research, automated data entry does have its disadvantages: (1) Data-collection equipment (a computer or terminal) might be obtrusive in the field environment; (2) administration by computer might be inconvenient or inappropriate (e.g., when a large group has access to only one terminal); and (3) data collected on one machine may not be transportable to another.

*Punched or Marked Cards*    Punched or marked cards are quite common in mainframe environments, but have been used only to a limited extent with microcomputers because the devices were too expensive for individual use. Recently, however, competition has forced down the price of some scanning machines and card readers to less than $1000. The most common interface with microcomputers is through mark-sensing card readers. Data are collected by marking (usually with a #2 pencil) preformatted sheets or cards, which are then read by the scanner or reader to create a data file.

There are advantages in using scanning devices or card readers for data input: (1) If data collection is administered through an objective paper-and-pencil task, cards or scan sheets can be easily adapted to many situations; (2) cards or sheets can be tabulated easily and quickly; (3) the same card reader can be linked to different comput-

## Card-Reader Software/Hardware

| Apple Family | Apple Macintosh | IBM PC |
| --- | --- | --- |
| Chatsworth OMR-2000 (hardware) Chatscore (software) Chatsworth Data Corp. 20710 Lassen St. Chatsworth, CA 91311 (800)423-5217 | ScanPro (works with Sentry 3000/Opscan 5 hardware by NCS and Scantron 8200 by Scantron, among others) Beach Tech Corp. P.O. Box Minneapolis, MN 55416 (800)733-3684 | Sentry 3000/Opscan 5 (hardware) Scan Tools (software) National Computer Systems 11000 Prairie Lakes Dr. P.O. Box 9365 Minneapolis, MN 55440 (800)359-3345 (612)829-3000 (MN) (800)668-8769 (Canada) |
| | | Scantron 8200 (hardware) Scanform (software) Scantron Corp. 1361 Valencia Avenue Tustin, CA 92680-6463 (800)SCANTRON |
| | | Chatsworth OMR-2000 (hardware) Chatscore (software) Chatsworth Data Corp. 20710 Lassen St. Chatsworth, CA 91311 (800)423-5217 |

ers, allowing the data to be transported; (4) a "hard" copy of the data can be archived to conform to many governmental storage requirements; and (5) subjects provide their own machine-readable data, which eliminates the need to employ coders.

Card or sheet readers are not perfect. They tend to be difficult to program and may require additional hardware to connect to a given computer. Moreover, the more sophisticated card readers generally require a modest investment of money, although once the investment is made, the machine can be used thousands of times with little maintenance.

*Optical Character Recognition*   A variant of card/mark sensing is optical character recognition (OCR), which is useful when text, or more specifically the text content, forms the variable(s) of interest (as in content analysis, for example), and the researcher is looking for a relatively quick and easy way to convert the text to computer-readable form for later analysis.

## Optical Character Recognition

| Apple Family | Apple Macintosh | IBM PC |
|---|---|---|
|  | OmniPage<br>Caere Corp.<br>100 Cooper Ct.<br>Los Gatos, CA 95030<br>(800)535-7226 | OmniPage 386<br>Caere Corp.<br>100 Cooper Court<br>Los Gatos, CA 95030<br>(800)535-7226 |
|  | Read-It!<br>Olduvai Corp.<br>7520 Red Rd., Ste. A<br>South Miami, FL 33143<br>(305)665-4665 | Wordscan Plus<br>Calera Recognition<br>Systems<br>2500 Augustine Dr.<br>Santa Clara, CA 95054<br>(408)986-8006 |
|  | TextScan<br>New Image Technology, Inc.<br>9701 Philadelphia Court<br>Lanham, MD 20706<br>(301)731-2000 | Recognize<br>Dest<br>1015 E. Brokaw Rd.<br>San Jose, CA 95131<br>(408)436-2700 |

With OCR, a page of text is placed on an optical scanner, which is attached to a computer. The scanner scans the document and the OCR software converts the bit-mapped patterns on the page to machine-readable text. The process takes anywhere from 30 seconds to two minutes per page and can be a tremendous time saver for the researcher who handles large amounts of text. Although the software recognition rate usually is very good (i.e., 95–99% accurate), it is not perfect, and the resultant computer file may require some editing after the scanning process is complete. In addition, the OCR software may be restricted as to the fonts it can recognize and the quality of the document which it can scan.

OCR software also can have a number of ancillary uses. For example, if the researcher wants to revise a non-computerized document, it generally is quicker to scan it and then edit the file than to retype the entire document. Similarly, OCR software can read data originally collected onto typewritten forms (e.g., personnel files) and convert them into a data set or database.

*Keying Data*    A fourth method of data entry is keying the data into a file through a data-management program. This is different from direct data entry in that the data collected on the paper-and-pencil instrument are entered into a computer file through the key-

## Keying Software

| Apple Family | Apple Macintosh | IBM PC |
|---|---|---|
| | | Keyentry III<br>Southern Computer<br>Systems, Inc.<br>2732 7th Ave. S.<br>Birmingham, AL 35233<br>(205)251-2985 |
| | | SPSS Data Entry II<br>SPSS, Inc.<br>444 N. Michigan Ave.<br>Chicago, IL 60611<br>(312)329-3300 |

board at a later time. Direct keying of data has several distinct advantages: (1) As is the case with mark-sense cards, data can be collected and coded on a separate data-collection instrument and subsequently entered into a microcomputer; and (2) no additional hardware is necessary to key the data. Disadvantages include: (1) Direct keying is a labor-intensive effort; human time is required to transcribe information from the collection instrument to machine-readable form; (2) data files created on one machine are not easily transportable to other machines; (3) data entered into one program often can be analyzed only by that program; and (4) errors can be made as the information is keyed. Most data-analysis packages come with some sort of keying facility, although there also are specialized programs to accomplish this task. Examples are given below.

## DATABASE-MANAGEMENT SOFTWARE

One method of data entry that can overcome many of the problems discussed above is the creation of a database. A more specialized use of database-management (DBM) software is illustrated in Chapter 2 in the discussion on generating a bibliographic database. One could create a specialized bibliographic database that uses generic DBM software in addition to the software mentioned in Chapter 2. In this section we discuss the use of DBM software for creating and maintaining information that subsequently will be analyzed through a quantitative or qualitative analysis program.

Information for most databases is input via the computer keyboard, but it also can be entered through external devices such as card readers or by direct data entry. Databases serve as a mechanism for data retrieval and manipulation. The major advantages of creating a database are: (1) Data can be input in many forms; (2) most DBM software has error-checking routines to ensure high data quality; (3) data can be transformed into various formats for subsequent use in a variety of analysis programs; (4) most DBM software calculates basic statistics and can generate nicely formatted reports; (5) the DBM software can be used for purposes other than data analysis; (6) the data are easy to update; and (7) DBM software provides a convenient way to archive data after use. Very·often, DBM files are self-documenting; that is, they are structured in such a way that the user can find out easily what is contained in the database.

The creation of a database is usually labor-intensive, and if its only purpose is data entry, then the benefits may not be worth the effort. In such cases, data-entry modules that come with most analy-

FIGURE 6.3.  Example of a Data-Entry Sheet in *FileMaker II* (Macintosh)

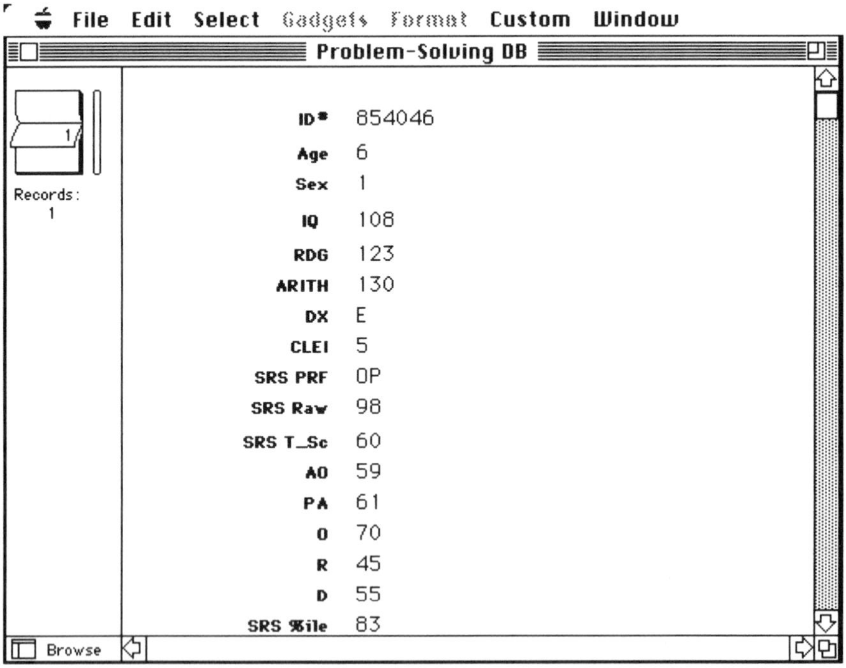

## Database Managers

| Apple Family | Apple Macintosh | IBM PC |
|---|---|---|
| DB Master Professional<br>Stone Edge Technologies<br>P.O. Box 200<br>Maple Glen, PA 19002<br>(215)641-1825 | Oracle for Macintosh<br>Oracle Corp.<br>20 Davis Dr.<br>Belmont, CA 94002<br>(415)598-8000 | Oracle<br>Oracle Corp.<br>20 Davis Dr.<br>Belmont, CA 94002<br>(415)598-8000 |
| Aladin<br>Advanced Data Institute<br>8001 Fruitridge Rd.<br>Sacramento, CA 95820<br>(916)381-8334 | Reflex Plus: The Database<br>Manager<br>Borland International<br>1800 Green Hills Rd.<br>Scotts Valley, CA 95066<br>(408)438-8400 | Reflex Plus: The Database<br>Manager<br>Borland International<br>1800 Green Hills Rd.<br>Scotts Valley, CA 95066<br>(408)438-8400 |
| AppleWorks<br>Claris Corp.<br>5201 Patrick Henry Dr.<br>P.O. Box 58168<br>Santa Clara, CA 95052<br>(800)544-8554 | Filemaker II<br>Claris Corp.<br>5201 Patrick Henry Dr.<br>P.O. Box 58168<br>Santa Clara, CA 95052<br>(800)544-8554 | dBase IV<br>Ashton-Tate<br>20101 Hamilton Ave.<br>Torrance, CA 90502<br>(213)329-8000 |
| Information Master<br>High Technology Software<br>Products, Inc.<br>8200 Classen Blvd.<br>Oklahoma City, OK 73146<br>(405)848-0480 | 4th Dimension<br>Acius, Inc.<br>10351 Bubb Rd.<br>Cupertino, CA 95014<br>(408)252-4444 | Foxbase+<br>Fox Software, Inc.<br>118 W. S. Boundary<br>Perrysburg, OH 43551<br>(419)874-0612 |
| Omnibase<br>Sourceview Software Int'l.<br>P.O. Box 578<br>Concord, CA 94522-0578<br>(415)686-8439 | MS File<br>Microsoft Corporation<br>16011 NE 36th Way<br>Box 97017<br>Redmond, WA 98073<br>(800)426-9400 | R:Base 5000<br>Microrim<br>3925 159th Ave., N.E.<br>Redmond, WA 98073<br>(206)885-2000 |

sis packages probably will be most helpful. A number of DBM packages interface directly with data-analysis counterparts. For example, *dBase IV*™, a popular MS-DOS-based DBM program, produces files which work quite nicely with *Abstat*™ for analysis or with *Lotus 1-2-3*™ for spreadsheet manipulation and graphics display.*

---

*\*Abstat* is produced by Anderson-Bell Corp., 11479 S. Pine Dr., Ste. 441, Parker, CO 80134. Phone: (408)841-9755. *Lotus 1-2-3* is produced by Lotus Development Corp., 55 Cambridge Parkway, Cambridge, MA 02142. Phone: (617)577-8500

DBM software works in a fashion similar to keying data into a forms-generation product. However, data manipulation generally is not possible with a forms-generation product, while with a DBM package, the researcher can apply extensive data-manipulation steps or create reports.

In *FileMaker II*, a popular DBM package for the Macintosh computer, the analyst creates a data-entry format consisting of descriptors of variables (e.g., the name of the variable, whether the data for that variable consist of text or numbers, the range of data, etc.) and the amount of form space dedicated for information on that variable. After the variable fields are created, data comprising the file are input either through direct keying or through an external device. Figure 6.3 shows an example of a simple database structure in *FileMaker II*.

As previously mentioned, creating a database is useful for research projects where the investigator has to update and manipulate the various forms of information that comprise the data collection effort. A psychologist might enter raw data from a test instrument into a database and then manipulate the raw data to come up with a useful score. Moreover, the psychologist could use the same database to generate a report of the test results for his or her records or to provide to another professional. Later, the information or test scores on all the clients could be exported to a data-analysis package for further study.

## DATA PREPARATION

Up to now we've described a number of data-input mechanisms and basic ways to manage the resulting data sets. With the possible exception of direct data entry, each mechanism is fallible and has the potential to introduce into the data set errors that ultimately could lead to incorrect conclusions by the researcher. There are, however, a few techniques that can be employed to ensure data integrity. Some of these are designed for data input via cards and are applicable to data entered via DBM software. The following discussion assumes that the researcher is constructing a "flat file" that has multiple lines or "cards" per observation. Like a spreadsheet, a "flat file" is a type of data matrix whereby observations of individuals are made as row entries and variables are arranged in columns. Figure 6.4 illustrates this concept.

In the example illustrated in Figure 6.4, there are two cards (or decks) per case with *n* variables. Case #001 refers to the information for the first person in the file. Deck #1, Case #001 means that infor-

FIGURE 6.4. Example of a "Flat" Data File with Multiple Lines
          per Case

| Case # | Deck # | Var #1 | . . . Var #n |
|--------|--------|--------|--------------|
| 001 | 1 | data | data |
| 001 | 2 | data | data |
| 002 | 2 | data | data |
| 003 | 1 | data | data |
| 003 | 2 | data | data |
| 002 | 1 | data | data |

mation on the card pertains to the first case number (001) and the
first "cardful" of data. It is quite possible for extensive data-
collection instruments to have more than 80 columns (i.e., one IBM
punchcard) of information. Deck #2, Case #001 is that information
from Case #001 which includes the second "cardful" of data.

### Sorting

With small studies it generally is an easy task to make sure that
all cards are in logical order. But take another look at Figure 6.4. You
will see that Deck #1, Case #002 is out of sequence. Ideally, we'd like
to have the file in the order shown in Figure 6.5.

Cards may be out of order for a variety of reasons. Perhaps in
the rush to get them to the card reader they were dropped. Perhaps
one was pulled for repunching. Or maybe one of the cards became
jammed while being read. Whatever the cause, the cards will need to

FIGURE 6.5. Example of a Resequenced Data File with Multiple Lines
          per Case

| Case # | Deck # | Var #1 | . . . Var #n |
|--------|--------|--------|--------------|
| 001 | 1 | data | data |
| 001 | 2 | data | data |
| 002 | 1 | data | data |
| 002 | 2 | data | data |
| 003 | 1 | data | data |
| 003 | 2 | data | data |

be sorted to get them back in their proper order. Fortunately, many data-analysis and database-management systems are equipped with software that can sort data easily and efficiently.

The sorting process is really quite simple. First the variable upon which sorting is based is identified. For data-management purposes, most sorts are based either on case or deck number. A first or outer sort might be made on case number, followed by a second or inner sort on deck number.

*Apple Interactive Data Analysis*™ (*AIDA*™), a data-analysis and preparation package for the Apple II, will permit the analyst to sort card images on one column at a time. Moreover, because the architecture of the program is open (it is written in BASIC), the user can modify the program easily to (1) sort on more than one variable; (2) sort on column widths wider than one; (3) sort alphabetic as well as numeric data; and (4) sort in ascending or descending order.

### Merge Checking

Occasionally the data structure of the information collected is not necessarily in the most efficient form for a microcomputer to process. For example, in Figure 6.5, the data-input structure consisted of two cards of information for each case. The restriction in the data structure was a function of data being punched onto cards or card images. Many programs allow you to rearrange the data-set structure to capitalize on the specific structure of the machine you happen to be using. Figure 6.6 shows our hypothetical data matrix changed to extend beyond the 80-column limit, thus making data storage more compact. A more compact storage algorithm may allow the researcher to process more cases, more variables, or both.

### Wild Code Checking

Many data-analysis programs allow the user to specify legitimate data ranges and subsequently instruct the data-analysis pack-

FIGURE 6.6. Example of a Merged Data File

| Case # | Deck # | VAR #1 | . . . Var #n | Case # | Deck # | Var #1 | . . . Var #n |
|--------|--------|--------|--------------|--------|--------|--------|--------------|
| 001 | 1 | data | data | 001 | 2 | data | data |
| 002 | 1 | data | data | 002 | 2 | data | data |
| 003 | 1 | data | data | 003 | 2 | data | data |

age to ensure that the data conform to the codebook specifications. It was mentioned earlier that some database applications automatically check for wild codes on data input. Moreover, this kind of checking occurs automatically on many direct data-input programs. However, once in a while the data analyst would like to make sure that a text or data file that was received over a network or through the mail is free of wild codes.

While *Systat* does not check for wild codes directly, it does allow the analyst to request an inventory of codes for each variable in the data set. Figure 6.7 shows how the researcher can generate a one-way frequency table for the variable "Grade" in the data set for our hypothetical study on the problem-solving strategies of children. One entry in the table that may seem odd is the grade "0." A check of the codebook reveals that this code represents those subjects who are either in preschool or kindergarten, so those codes are not classified as being "wild."

Now that the data have been checked for errors, we're ready to go on to the next step—data analysis. While data management can be rather dull and mechanical, it can go a long way toward preserving the accuracy of statistical results.

FIGURE 6.7. Example of Output from a Selection in the Systat 5.0 Menu to Create a Frequency Table for Data Inspection (Macintosh)

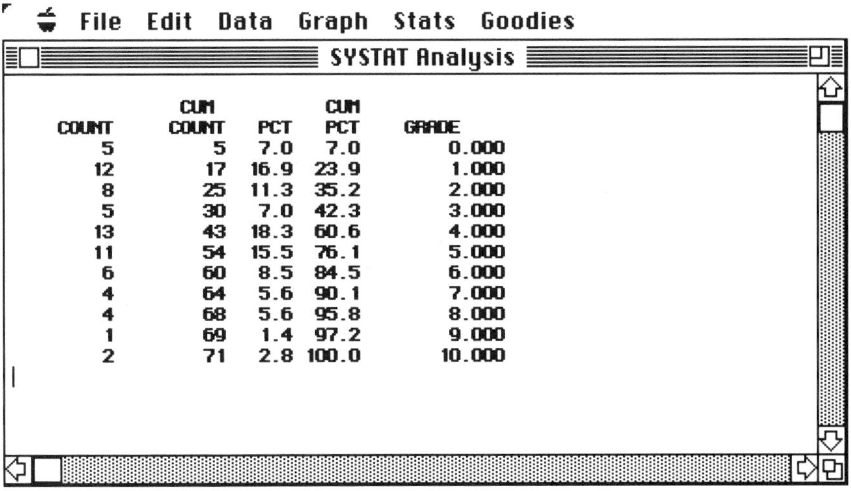

**File   Edit   Data   Graph   Stats   Goodies**

**═══════════════════════ SYSTAT Analysis ═══════════════**

| COUNT | CUM COUNT | PCT | CUM PCT | GRADE |
|-------|-----------|-----|---------|--------|
| 5 | 5 | 7.0 | 7.0 | 0.000 |
| 12 | 17 | 16.9 | 23.9 | 1.000 |
| 8 | 25 | 11.3 | 35.2 | 2.000 |
| 5 | 30 | 7.0 | 42.3 | 3.000 |
| 13 | 43 | 18.3 | 60.6 | 4.000 |
| 11 | 54 | 15.5 | 76.1 | 5.000 |
| 6 | 60 | 8.5 | 84.5 | 6.000 |
| 4 | 64 | 5.6 | 90.1 | 7.000 |
| 4 | 68 | 5.6 | 95.8 | 8.000 |
| 1 | 69 | 1.4 | 97.2 | 9.000 |
| 2 | 71 | 2.8 | 100.0 | 10.000 |

## ANALYZE DATA AND INTERPRET RESULTS

In this section, the use of the microcomputer to analyze data is explored. Although the emphasis is on quantitative analysis, qualitative analysis (i.e., content analysis) is discussed toward the end of the chapter. It is beyond the scope of this book to explore all of the statistical packages currently available for microcomputers. The number of packages is growing by leaps and bounds. Even as the authors were putting this book together, four major packages were introduced. In general, the quality of the packages is improving, but they still vary greatly in price and performance. Comprehensive comparisons of many statistical-analysis packages can be found in Carpenter and Morganstein (1984); Fridlund (1988); Lachenbruch (1983); and Raskin (1989).

One important thing to keep in mind when looking for a statistical package is whether you would ever have to transfer your data from floppy disk to a mainframe or minicomputer. The need to transfer data to a larger computer can arise for two reasons: (1) your study design calls for a statistic which can be calculated only on a mainframe statistical package; (2) the size of your sample exceeds the memory capacity of your microcomputer. While these restrictions have been important in the past, we have found that today's microcomputer data-analysis packages rival those on the mainframe for comprehensiveness, and that restrictions of sample size are limited to the size of your microcomputer's hard disk and usually not to the processing capacity of the CPU. Moreover, we can state unequivocally that almost all microcomputer data-analysis packages are easier to use than their mainframe counterparts. Several packages, such as *SPSS/PC+*® and *SAS*®, have built-in telecommunications modules to facilitate transferring data to and from the mainframe computer.

Looking for relationships is natural in social science research. It has become increasingly important not only to test for differences in groups, characterize relationships, and identify factors, but also to search and analyze data for trends. Until now, trend analysis has not been used widely, partly because extra information must be added to existing data sets in order to obtain trends. Often the information printed out has seemed obtuse and difficult to interpret. Further, graphing the necessary values has been difficult on a large mainframe computer. Hence, the researcher has had to rely on numerical values rather than graphs to indicate a trend, thus losing the "picture" often needed to explore data. The microcomputer not only overcomes these drawbacks, but has advantages of its own. First, the graphics capabilities that most microcomputers support offer resolution that is clear enough to illustrate trends, if any are present. Second, the ease of adapting and manipulating data sets encourages the search for trends. Third, the microcomputer can be used to compare several kinds of analyses so that the researcher gets a real feel for the structure and implications inherent in the data.

There are some drawbacks of using microcomputers to analyze data. First, the size of the data set may be limited, although lately this has been overcome by increased disk capacities and by a technique called "overlaying," where only a part of a program or data set is in memory at one time. Second, the time required to run analyses often is greater than on a large mainframe. Often the researcher has to think in terms of "cup of coffee" units of time rather than seconds. Third, there is a lack of uniform data-entry techniques. Overall, the user's ability to easily modify programs and to understand and modify analysis techniques, plus the friendly nature of the machines, outweigh the problems of using microcomputers to analyze data.

In the following discussion we:

1. Use a microcomputer to examine a data set by means of exploratory data-analysis techniques.
2. Use a microcomputer to analyze data by traditional techniques.
3. Indicate features that the analyst should keep in mind when evaluating alternative packages.

### Exploratory Data Analysis

A good way to begin analyzing data is to visualize the structure of your information. For univariate analyses, you might start by generating a histogram or stem-and-leaf plot to examine the distribution of the variable. Many inferential statistics assume that a dependent variable is normally distributed. In addition, the form of a variable can provide information about the effectiveness of an intervention. A peaked distribution might show that there was a homogeneous response to the experimental manipulation, while a flatter distribution might show that some subjects reacted very positively to the intervention while others did not. Figure 6.8 shows the *Systat* output for a histogram of the variable reading achievement (RDG) from the data set of our hypothetical study on problem solving, and Figure 6.9 illustrates the stem-and-leaf plot for the same data.*

*Thanks to Dr. Louis A. Chandler, University of Pittsburgh, for providing these data.

FIGURE 6.8. Example of Output from a Histogram in *Systat* 5.0
for the Variable "Reading Achievement" (RDG)

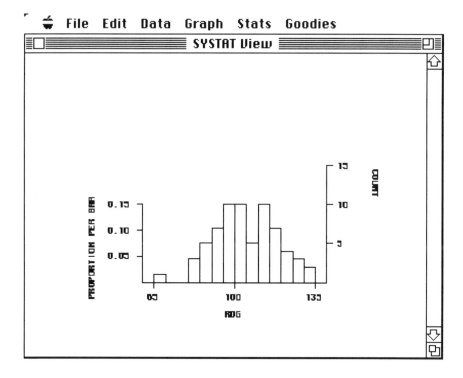

*Systat* also enables the analyst to create a probability plot which graphs raw score values against standardized expected score values. This technique shows how far from normal the data actually are. A normally distributed variable will generate a straight line, starting in the lower left corner and proceeding to the upper right portion of the graph. Figure 6.10 presents this information for the reading-achievement variable (RDG). Formal statistics on skewness and kurtosis also can be obtained by selecting those options from the "Stats" menu.

On the evidence of our exploratory analysis, we might conclude that the variable RDG is approximately normally distributed.

The visual techniques discussed thus far relate to inspecting the normality of single variables. But what about the relationship between two variables or among more than two variables? There are several exploratory techniques that can be used in these situations. For example, what is the nature of the relationships among the variables RDG (reading achievement), ART (arithmetic achievement), and

FIGURE 6.9. Example of Output from a Stem-and-Leaf
            Plot in Systat 5.0 for the Variable
            "Reading Achievement" (RDG)

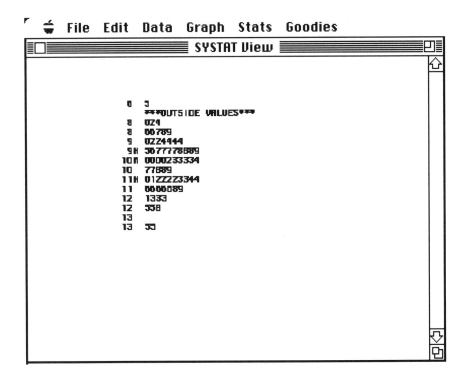

IQ? We would expect them to be generally positive; that is, an individual who scores high on the IQ variable would be expected to perform well on the two measures of achievement. One initial step that might be taken is to create a scattergram or bivariate scatter plot for each pair of variables, but this would show only one set of relationships at a time and would be somewhat tedious to produce. An alternate approach is to generate a scatterplot matrix (SPLOM) in *Systat*. A SPLOM plot might be thought of as the visual analog of a correlation matrix, simultaneously showing the bivariate relationship among multiple variables. The SPLOM plot displayed in Figure 6.11 reveals that our initial suspicions are correct—by and large, there is a positive relationship among all three selected variables.

Yet another way to see the relationships among the three variables is to produce a three-dimensional spin plot. The 3D spin plot essentially represents three variables on separate axes, with one vi-

FIGURE 6.10.  Example of Output from a Probability
Plot in *Systat* 5.0 for the Variable
Reading Achievement'' (RDG)

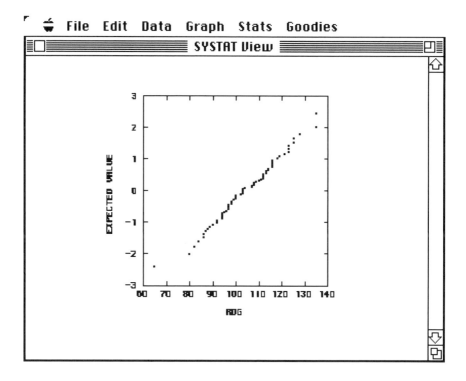

sual plane. To change the visual perspective, the analyst can rotate or
spin one or more of the axes to get the best view of the data structure.
Figures 6.12 and 6.13 show two views of a 3D spin plot produced with
*Systat*, one before spinning and one after. These views tend to reinforce our hunches about the linearly positive relationships among
the variables.

### Descriptive Statistics

As the term implies, descriptive statistics describe, tabulate, or
depict specific objects.  Information provided graphically allows the
researcher to visualize the structure of the data, but has little utility
for formal hypothesis testing. Generally, researchers calculate sample statistics and employ inferential tests to determine whether or
not the data were drawn from a given population. For our hypotheti-

FIGURE 6.11. Example of Output from a SPLOM Plot in *Systat* 5.0
for the Variables "IQ," "Reading Achievement"
(RDG), and "Arithmetic Achievement" (ART)

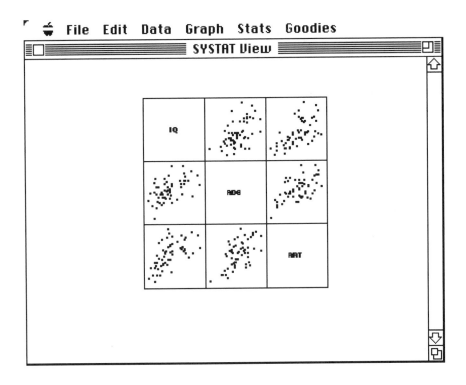

cal study, we might begin by asking the following questions: What is the average IQ of our sample? How variable is it? What is its relationship to other variables? Again, *Systat* can help us answer these questions. Figure 6.14 provides the output of a typical first step in reducing quantitative information, a frequency distribution. The frequency distribution simply lists the frequency of observations within a specific score interval. Notice that the frequency distribution is conceptually similar to its visual analog, the histogram.

As a next step, we may wish to calculate measures of central tendency and variability for a subset of our variables. Figure 6.15 displays the output of a request for these statistics. Our sample data become more interesting when we learn that, for all three measures (IQ, Reading Achievement, Arithmetic Achievement), the mean of the test-standardization sample was about 100 and the standard deviation was about 15.

FIGURE 6.12. One View of Output from a 3D Spin Plot in *Systat*
5.0 For the Variables "IQ," "Reading Achievement"
(RDG), and "Arithmetic Achievement" (ART)

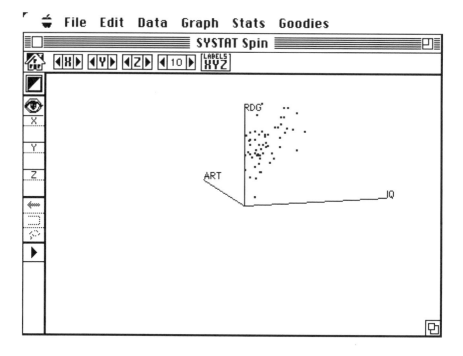

The exploratory analysis illustrated a modest positive correlation among the three measures, but did not statistically summarize the nature of that relationship. We can use *Systat* to calculate the Pearson Product Moment Correlation as a way to express statistically the direction and magnitude of the linear relationship. Figure 6.16 shows a correlation and probability matrix consisting of the three measures, IQ, Reading Achievement, and Arithmetic Achievement. This analysis was generated easily from *Systat*'s "Stats" menu under the selection of "Correlation." Within the "Correlation" submenu were choices related to different types of correlation statistics. For the present analysis, the "Pearson" alternative was selected.

If we were formally testing null hypotheses (e.g., that there are no relationships among the three variables), two types of probability matrices could be generated with *Systat*. One probability takes into account the number of hypotheses being tested (i.e., a significance level formulated with the Bonferroni inequality), and another as-

FIGURE 6.13. Another View of the Same Output from a 3D Spin
Plot in *Systat* 5.0. Perspective has changed
as a result of "spinning" the data.

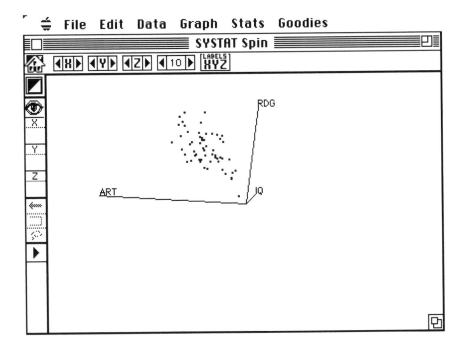

sumes that the test being performed is based only on one hypothesis. Even when the conservative Bonferroni inequality (calculated in Figure 6.16) is used, we would conclude that our variables are significantly related.

The data we have been using as an example have had the psychometric properties of data at the interval scale and have been summarized as such. However, our data set also contains discrete (nominally scaled) data, which may be aggregated in different ways. For example, Figure 6.17 illustrates the output of a bivariate frequency (two-way) table consisting of the variables Sex, where 0 = female and 1 = male, and Clinical Diagnosis (DX$),* where E = emotional problem, L = learning problem, and N = no problem. Al-

---

*Sytsat makes distinctions between numeric and alphanumeric variables. Some analyses assume that data are in numeric form, regardless of how they are used. Alphanumeric data are designated with a $ after the variable name.

FIGURE 6.14. Partial View of a Frequency-Distribution Table for the Variable "Reading Achievement" (RDG) in *Systat* 5.0

File Edit Data Graph Stats Goodies

SYSTAT Analysis

TABLE OF VALUES FOR RDG

FREQUENCIES

| . | 65.000 | 80.000 | 82.000 | 84.000 | 86.000 |
|---|---|---|---|---|---|
| 4 | 1 | 1 | 1 | 1 | 2 |

| 87.000 | 88.000 | 89.000 | 90.000 | 92.000 | 94.000 |
|---|---|---|---|---|---|
| 1 | 1 | 1 | 1 | 2 | 4 |

| 95.000 | 96.000 | 97.000 | 98.000 | 99.000 | 100.000 |
|---|---|---|---|---|---|
| 1 | 1 | 4 | 3 | 1 | 4 |

FIGURE 6.15. Descriptive Statistics for the Variables "IQ," "Reading Achievement" (RDG), and "Artithmetic Achievement" (ART) in *Systat* 5.0

File Edit Data Graph Stats Goodies

SYSTAT Analysis

TOTAL OBSERVATIONS: 71

| | IQ | RDG | ART |
|---|---|---|---|
| N OF CASES | 71 | 67 | 67 |
| MINIMUM | 84.000 | 65.000 | 69.000 |
| MAXIMUM | 144.000 | 135.000 | 135.000 |
| MEAN | 109.338 | 104.537 | 103.836 |
| VARIANCE | 201.084 | 189.101 | 240.957 |
| STANDARD DEV | 14.180 | 13.751 | 15.523 |

FIGURE 6.16. Correlation and Probability Matrix for the Variables
"IQ," "Reading Achievement" (RDG), and
"Arithmetic Achievement" (ART) in *Systat* 5.0

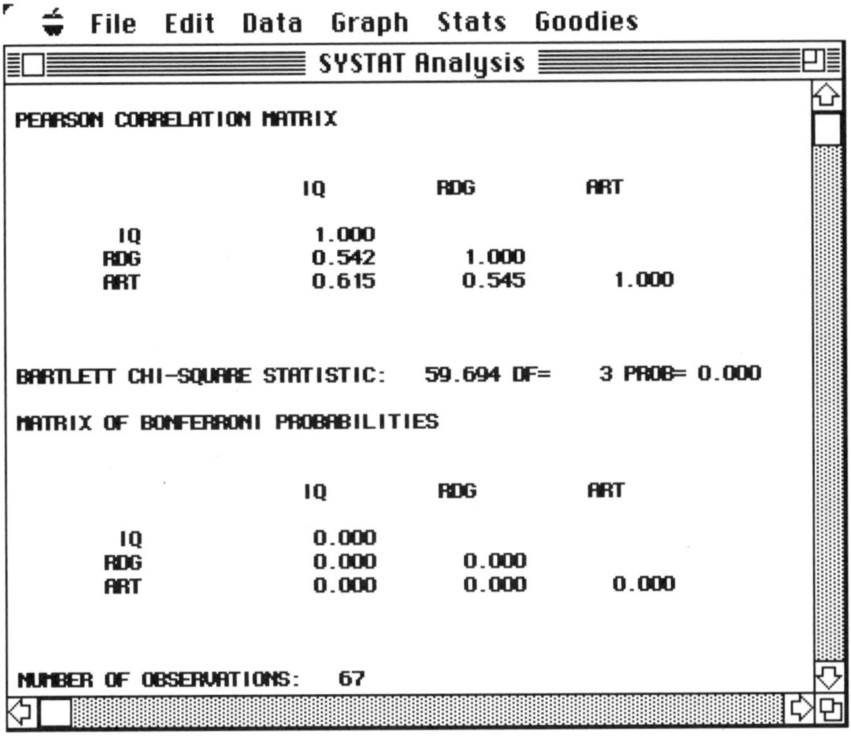

```
r  ⛴  File   Edit   Data   Graph   Stats   Goodies
┌─────────────────────── SYSTAT Analysis ───────────────────────┐
│                                                                │
│ PEARSON CORRELATION MATRIX                                     │
│                                                                │
│                  IQ          RDG          ART                  │
│                                                                │
│     IQ          1.000                                          │
│     RDG         0.542       1.000                              │
│     ART         0.615       0.545       1.000                  │
│                                                                │
│                                                                │
│ BARTLETT CHI-SQUARE STATISTIC:    59.694 DF=    3 PROB= 0.000  │
│                                                                │
│ MATRIX OF BONFERRONI PROBABILITIES                             │
│                                                                │
│                  IQ          RDG          ART                  │
│                                                                │
│     IQ          0.000                                          │
│     RDG         0.000       0.000                              │
│     ART         0.000       0.000       0.000                  │
│                                                                │
│                                                                │
│ NUMBER OF OBSERVATIONS:    67                                  │
└────────────────────────────────────────────────────────────────┘
```

though the sample is very small, one can't help wondering why males comprise six of the seven cases of children with diagnosed learning problems (L). *Systat*'s extended output allows us to formally test the null hypothesis that Sex is unrelated to Clinical Diagnosis.

## Inferential Statistics

Inferential statistics allow the researcher to formally test hypotheses concerning population parameters. Is the mean Reading Achievement the same for females as it is for males? Are IQ, Number of Stressful Life Events, and Sex significant predictors of Arithmetic Achievement? We can combine the use of the design of our study and

FIGURE 6.17. Partial Output of a Bivariate Frequency (Two-way)
Table for the Variables "Sex" and "DX$"
(Clinical Diagnosis) in *Systat* 5.0

```
 r  ≜ File  Edit  Data  Graph  Stats  Goodies
▤□▒▒▒▒▒▒▒▒▒▒▒▒▒▒▒▒▒▒▒▒ SYSTAT Analysis ▒▒▒▒▒▒▒▒▒▒▒▒▒▒▒▒▒▒▒□▤
 TABLE OF      SEX      (ROWS) BY        DX$    (COLUMNS)

 FREQUENCIES

                 E        L        N       TOTAL
             ──────────────────────────
    0.000        17        1        3        21

    1.000        36        6        0        42

 TOTAL           53        7        3        63


 WARNING: MORE THAN ONE-FIFTH OF FITTED CELLS ARE SPARSE (FREQUENCY < 5)
 SIGNIFICANCE TESTS ARE SUSPECT


 TEST STATISTIC                      VALUE        DF        PROB
   PEARSON CHI-SQUARE                7.181         2       0.028
   LIKELIHOOD RATIO CHI-SQUARE       7.951         2       0.019
```

inferential statistics to base generalizations about a population on
sample data. The ability to make these generalizations is a very powerful feature of probabilistic statistics.

*Systat* allows the researcher to use a host of inferential statistics in analyzing data. For example, suppose we wanted to answer the
first question above: "Is the mean Reading Achievement the same for
females as it is for males?" We might consider using an independent
*t*-test to answer this question. *Systat* generates a *t*-test from the
"Stats" menu. All the researcher has to do is identify the dependent
variable and the independent variable, and click the mouse button.
Figure 6.18 displays the output from this analysis.

The results are somewhat interesting in that the conclusion one
reaches (at the .05 alpha level*) might change as a function of the formula used to calculate the student's *t* statistic. If the "separate variances" formula (used when the variances appear to be quite
different) were chosen, then the null hypothesis would be rejected

---

*Systat* prints out exact *p*-values or allows the user to specify confidence bounds
in situations where appropriate.

FIGURE 6.18.  Student's *t*-test with "Reading Achievement"
(RDG) as the Dependent Variable and "Sex"
as the Independent Variable, from the
*Systat* 5.0 "Stats" Submenu

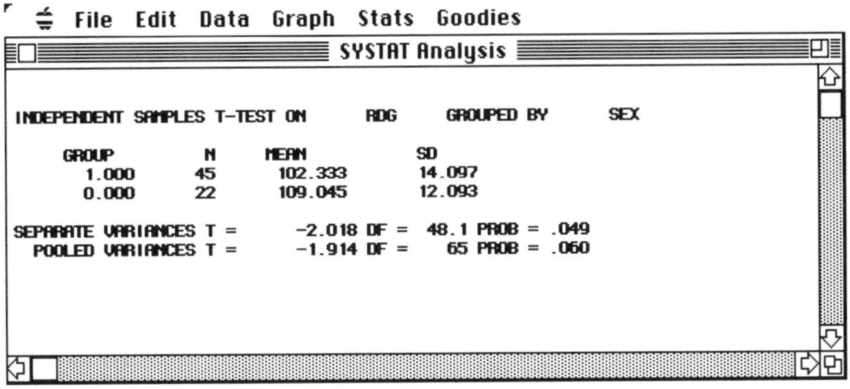

```
 ⬥  File  Edit  Data  Graph  Stats  Goodies
▦◻▦▦▦▦▦▦▦▦▦▦▦▦▦▦ SYSTAT Analysis ▦▦▦▦▦▦▦▦▦▦▦▦▦▦◻▦
                                                                        ⇧
  INDEPENDENT SAMPLES T-TEST ON      RDG      GROUPED BY      SEX

       GROUP        N      MEAN           SD
       1.000        45     102.333        14.097
       0.000        22     109.045        12.093

  SEPARATE VARIANCES T =      -2.018 DF =   48.1 PROB = .049
  POOLED VARIANCES T =        -1.914 DF =     65 PROB = .060

                                                                        ⇩
◁▏▦▦▦▦▦▦▦▦▦▦▦▦▦▦▦▦▦▦▦▦▦▦▦▦▦▦▦▦▦▦▦▦▦▦▦▦▦▦▦▦▦▦▦▦▦▦▦  ⇨▢
```

and we would conclude that males and females do differ with respect
to levels of reading achievement. Alternatively, if we were to choose
to use the "pooled variances" formula (probably the more reasonable
choice in this instance), then the null hypothesis of no gender differences would be retained.

Often the researcher's questions are very complex, involving
more than one dependent variable. This situation would call for multivariate analysis, which can be quite intimidating to the researcher.
Although *Systat* can't simplify the intricacies of complex designs, it
does take a number of steps toward making their analysis easier.
Let's say, for example, that instead of just focusing on Arithmetic
Achievement, we wanted to know whether Academic Achievement
differed between males and females. Academic Achievement might
be defined as an index or vector of both Arithmetic Achievement
(ART) and Reading Achievement (RDG). Of course, we could perform
separate *t*-tests on each dependent variable, but generating multiple
*t*-tests would increase the likelihood of making a Type 1 error. Moreover, we may believe that the vector of dependent variables is a more
valid measure of the hypothetical construct than each dependent
variable taken separately. The analysis we might choose is a multivariate *t*-test, or *F*-test, which is available under the "MGLH" (Multivariate General Linear Hypothesis) submenu within *Systat*'s "Stats"
menu. With this procedure, the analyst simply identifies for the pro-

FIGURE 6.19.  Partial Output from a Multivariate *t*-test with
"Reading Achievement" (RDG) and "Arithmetic
Achievement" (ART) as the Dependent Variables
and "Sex" as the Independent Variable, from
the *Systat* 5.0 "MGLH" Submenu

```
 ⌘  File  Edit  Data  Graph  Stats  Goodies
▤□▤▤▤▤▤▤▤▤▤▤▤▤▤▤▤ SYSTAT Analysis ▤▤▤▤▤▤▤▤▤▤▤▤▤▤▤□▤
UNIVARIATE F TESTS                                                        ⇧

     VARIABLE       SS        DF       MS            F           P

       RDG       665.702       1     665.702       3.662       0.060
       ERROR   11814.955      65     181.769
       ART      1745.803       1    1745.803       8.015       0.006
       ERROR   14157.391      65     217.806

MULTIVARIATE TEST STATISTICS

          WILKS' LAMBDA =     0.887
          F-STATISTIC =       4.093   DF =   2,  64     PROB =      0.021

          PILLAI TRACE =      0.113
          F-STATISTIC =       4.093   DF =   2,  64     PROB =      0.021

  HOTELLING-LAWLEY TRACE =    0.128
          F-STATISTIC =       4.093   DF =   2,  64     PROB =      0.021 ⇩
◁▯▯▯▯▯▯▯▯▯▯▯▯▯▯▯▯▯▯▯▯▯▯▯▯▯▯▯▯▯▯▯▯▯▯▯▯▯▯▯▯▯▯▯▯▯▯▯▯▯ ▷▣
```

gram the dependent variables, the independent variable(s), and the covariate(s), if any.* Figure 6.19 illustrates the output from this multivariate analysis.

The multivariate test statistics reveal a significant difference between males and females on Academic Achievement, defined as the vector of RDG and ART. Post hoc analysis shows that the difference is significant on ART, with females performing better than males, but nonsignificant on RDG. Notice that the output for univariate tests is provided as well. The probability level calculated for the univariate *F*-test on RDG is the same as that for the "pooled variances" *t*-test calculated in Figure 6.18. The program uses the "pooled variances" formula because one of the assumptions underlying multivariate analysis is that the variances within each group are equal. *Systat* output provides information as to whether or not that assumption is tenable.

Now suppose we wish to answer the second question: "Are IQ, Number of Stressful Life Events, and Sex significant predictors of Arithmetic Achievement?" In this example, Number of Stressful Life

*Systat* allows additional options as well.

Events is operationalized as the score on Chandler's (1985) *Children's Life Events Inventory* (CLEI). In order to answer this question, we might wish to consider multiple regression as a possible analytic technique. The analysis assumes that all the independent variables and the dependent variable are at the interval scale, normally distributed, and that observations were selected independently. Up to now, we have treated Sex as a nominally scaled variable, but because it is coded dichotomously (0,1), it possesses all the properties of an intervally scaled variable.* Dichotomously scored variables sometimes are called "dummy variables" in multiple regression. Multiple regression is generated from the "MGLH" submenu in *Systat*. As before, performing the analysis is as easy as identifying the independent variables, the dependent variable, and clicking "OK," although the program does allow the analyst to configure special model constraints (e.g., a standardized multiple regression or a model with multiplicative terms).

Figure 6.20 illustrates the output for our example. The multiple-regression model significantly predicts Arithmetic Achievement (ART) scores, explaining almost 45 percent of the variance in the sample and about 41 percent of the variance in the population. Two of the predictors, IQ and Sex, were identified as contributing significantly to the overall model. The output from the regression table, as well as from all the previous analyses, could be copied easily and placed directly into a report or article.

Sometimes the assumptions underlying the use of parametric inferential statistics cannot be met. For example, an examination of the distribution of the dependent variable may show that it is highly skewed, or the dependent variable may be ordinally scaled. In such a situation, the analyst can choose to use nonparametric statistics. *Systat* also supports many of the popular nonparametric statistical techniques in its "NPAR" selection from the "Stats" menu. One popular nonparametric analysis is the Kruskal-Wallis test, a nonparametric analog of one-way analysis of variance. In our example, illustrated in Figure 6.21, the dependent variable is the percentile ranking on the *Stress Response Scale* (Chandler, 1983), a measure of stress outcomes, and the independent variable is Sex. The research question here might be, "Do males and females differ with respect to level of stress outcomes?" We have chosen to use the nonparametric technique because percentile rankings typically are treated as ordinally scaled statistics. On this analysis, we retain the null hypothesis and

---

*Actually, a dichotomously scored variable maintains the properties of a ratio-scaled number with a true zero point.

FIGURE 6.20.  Partial Output from a Multiple Regression with "Arithmetic Achievement" (ART) as the Dependent Variable and "Children's Life Events Inventory" (CLEI), "IQ," and "Sex" (dummy variable) as the Independent Variables, from the *Systat* 5.0 "MGLH" Submenu

```
  File  Edit  Data  Graph  Stats  Goodies
≡□≡≡≡≡≡≡≡≡≡≡≡≡≡≡≡ SYSTAT Analysis ≡≡≡≡≡≡≡≡≡≡≡≡≡≡≡≡≡
  4 CASES DELETED DUE TO MISSING DATA.

DEP VAR:    ART     N:    67   MULTIPLE R:  .665  SQUARED MULTIPLE R:   .443
ADJUSTED SQUARED MULTIPLE R:  .416    STANDARD ERROR OF ESTIMATE:    11.861

 VARIABLE    COEFFICIENT   STD ERROR   STD COEF  TOLERANCE    T    P(2 TAIL)

CONSTANT       45.372      12.284       0.000        .       3.694    0.000
   CLEI        -0.366       0.369      -0.098     0.909     -0.991    0.325
    IQ          0.612       0.102       0.571     0.970      5.983    0.000
   SEX         -6.897       3.262      -0.210     0.895     -2.115    0.038


                        ANALYSIS OF VARIANCE

  SOURCE    SUM-OF-SQUARES   DF   MEAN-SQUARE    F-RATIO      P

REGRESSION     7040.664      3     2346.888     16.683     0.000
 RESIDUAL      8862.530     63      140.675
```

FIGURE 6.21.  Kruskal-Wallis Test with "Stress Response Scale Percentile Rank" (SRS__ILE) as the Dependent Variable and "Sex" as the Independent Variable, from the *Systat* 5.0 "NPAR" Submenu

```
  File  Edit  Data  Graph  Stats  Goodies
≡□≡≡≡≡≡≡≡≡≡≡≡≡≡≡≡ SYSTAT Analysis ≡≡≡≡≡≡≡≡≡≡≡≡≡≡≡≡≡

KRUSKAL-WALLIS ONE-WAY ANALYSIS OF VARIANCE FOR  71 CASES
  DEPENDENT VARIABLE IS   SRS_ILE
  GROUPING VARIABLE IS      SEX

  GROUP     COUNT    RANK SUM

   0.000      23      964.500
   1.000      48     1591.500


MANN-WHITNEY U TEST STATISTIC =     688.500
PROBABILITY IS       0.092
CHI-SQUARE APPROXIMATION =      2.837 WITH    1 DF
```

conclude that males and females do not differ with respect to their observed levels of stress.

A final example concludes our section on quantitative analysis. Often the researcher may wish to explore the data structure of a newly developed instrument or examine how a new instrument relates to a battery of other instruments. A number of statistical techniques exist for this purpose, such as cluster analysis, multidimensional scaling, and factor analysis. All of these techniques are available in *Systat*. Moreover, *Systat* has developed a supplementary software package called *E-Z Path*™, which works with Systat data sets and allows the analyst to formally test hypotheses concerning the structure of data. *E-Z Path* performs a covariance structure analysis much like that done in *LISREL VI*™ (Jöreskog & Sörbom, 1984) and provides estimates of relationship parameters as well as goodness-of-fit statistics.

Because exploring the structure of data is based on correlational analysis, it is necessary to have a large number of observations relative to the number of variables used.* For this reason, we shift from our hypothetical study of problem-solving strategies to an analysis of the Anxiety Stress Index (ASI) (Peterson & Reiss, 1987), a 16-item instrument designed to measure "state" anxiety.† The data for this example of factor analysis were drawn from Telch, Shermis, and Lucas (1989), who were concerned about the unidimensional nature of the ASI.‡ To investigate this question, data were gathered from 840 subjects. A subset of the results of a principal-components analysis with varimax rotation is presented in Figure 6.22. Although the data set is relatively large (16 variables and 840 cases), *Systat* was able to compute the principal-components analysis with varimax rotation in under five minutes. Just ten years ago, using another analysis package, a smaller data set, and a third-generation computer, we would enter our analysis parameters on the computer before going to bed at night and hope the analysis would be finished before we went off to work the next morning.

The analysis shows a relatively weak first factor. Moreover, there is some doubt as to whether the ASI measures a unitary construct (Telch, Shermis, & Lucas, 1989).

---

*With small samples, minor shifts in data values can produce relatively large differences in correlations.

†The distinction here is one of "state" versus "trait" anxiety. State anxiety is thought of as a more temporal or acute form of anxiety, whereas trait anxiety is thought to be more permanent or chronic.

‡Thanks to Dr. Michael Telch, The University of Texas at Austin, for providing these data.

FIGURE 6.22.  Partial Output from a Factor Analysis of
Statements on the Anxiety Sensitivity Index (*N*
= 840), from the *Systat* 5.0 "FACTOR"
Submenu

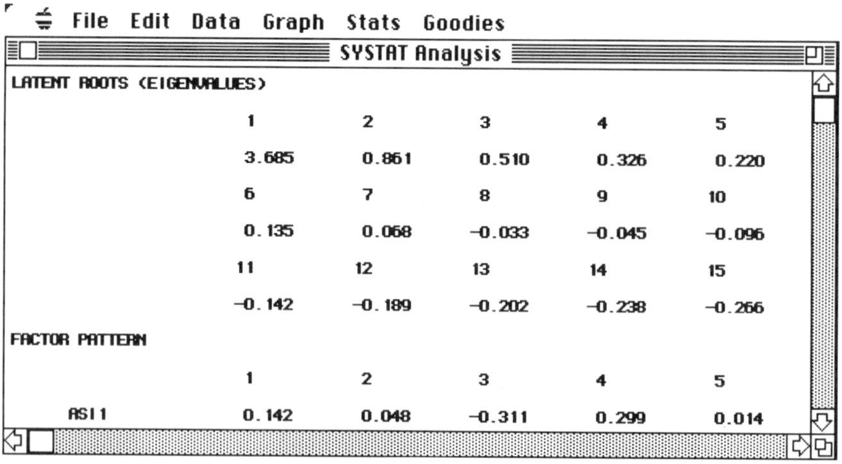

 File  Edit  Data  Graph  Stats  Goodies

=== SYSTAT Analysis ===

LATENT ROOTS (EIGENVALUES)

| 1 | 2 | 3 | 4 | 5 |
|---|---|---|---|---|
| 3.685 | 0.861 | 0.510 | 0.326 | 0.220 |

| 6 | 7 | 8 | 9 | 10 |
|---|---|---|---|---|
| 0.135 | 0.068 | -0.033 | -0.045 | -0.096 |

| 11 | 12 | 13 | 14 | 15 |
|---|---|---|---|---|
| -0.142 | -0.189 | -0.202 | -0.238 | -0.266 |

FACTOR PATTERN

| | 1 | 2 | 3 | 4 | 5 |
|---|---|---|---|---|---|
| ASI 1 | 0.142 | 0.048 | -0.311 | 0.299 | 0.014 |

## TEXT ANALYSIS

Before ending this chapter, it would be useful to acknowledge that
not all data can be linked to quantitative indices. While the application of statistics has the desirable property of reducing a vast
amount of information to a few (one hopes) comprehensible numbers, some social science studies are not amenable to this type of
analysis. For example, in communications research, a content analysis may not be so concerned with how often the word "software"
shows up in a magazine, but rather in what contexts or under what
conditions it is used. Microcomputers can help with this type of
study as well.

As we discussed earlier in this chapter, Optical Character Recognition (OCR) software may be used to input textual data. For example, if a researcher was interested in analyzing trends in the
microcomputer industry, a base of knowledge might be derived from
magazines oriented toward microcomputer news (although some
pundits might argue this point). Articles from the magazines would
be scanned and saved as text files on a floppy or hard disk. Once the
text was entered, a number of different packages could be used to
analyze it.

## Data Analysis Packages for Mainframe/Mini Computers

| Apple Family | Apple Macintosh | IBM PC |
|---|---|---|
| Apple Interactive Data Analysis (AIDA) Action Research Northwest 11442 Marine View Dr. S.W. Seattle. WA 98146 (206)241-1645 | Systat Systat, Inc. 1800 Sherman Ave. Evanston, IL 60201 (708)864-5670 | Systat Systat, Inc. 1800 Sherman Ave. Evanston, IL 60201 (708)864-5670 |
| Statistics with Finesse P.O. Box 339 Fayetteville, AR 72702 (501)521-7278 | SPSS/Mac SPSS, Inc. 444 N. Michigan Ave. Chicago, IL 60611 (312)329-3300 | SPSS-PC+ SPSS, Inc. 444 N. Michigan Ave. Chicago, IL 60611 (312)329-3300 |
| Stats Plus Human System Dynamics 9010 Reseda Blvd., Ste. 222 Northridge, CA 91324 (818)993-8536 | JMP SAS Institute Inc. P.O. Box 8000 SAS Circle Cary, NC 27512-8000 (919)677-8123 | SAS SAS Institute Inc. P.O. Box 8000 SAS Circle Cary, NC 27512-8000 (919)677-8123 |
| A-Stat 83 Rosen Grandon Associates, Inc. 3106 Edgewater Dr. Greensboro, NC 27403 (916)292-2116 | StatView SE+ Graphics StatView II SuperAnova Abacus Concepts, Inc. 1984 Bonita Ave. Berkeley, CA 94704 (415)540-0260 | BMDP BMDP Statistical Software, Inc. 1440 Sepulveda Blvd., Ste. 316 Los Angeles, CA 90025 (213)479-7799 |

A traditional approach to performing a content analysis is to do word, phrase, or "concept" counts, as mentioned above. That is, the researcher identifies the number of times a word, phrase, or concept appears in a piece of communication. Many word processors have built-in tools to do this. For example, our word processors can count the number of words in a document (e.g., this chapter has approximately 7400 words up to this point—you can be sure that we did not count them ourselves!). We can also use the "search" function of our word processors (or databases, for that matter) to do a count of the number of times "OCR" appears (8 times). Another analysis might consist of creating ratios (e.g., 8/7400) of appearance of a concept to the total amount of communication.

Dedicated content-analysis packages usually are quite sophisticated in their approach. Often they enable the researcher to link specific communications to a higher level of abstraction. In the example

FIGURE 6.23.  View of a Map in *ArchiText* 1.0 (Macintosh)

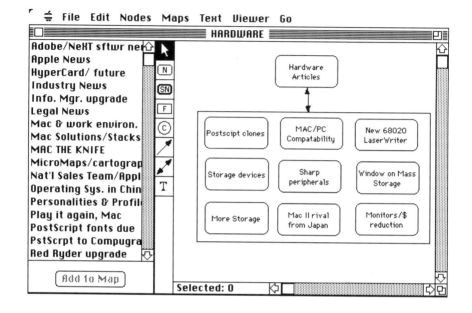

shown in Figure 6.23, *ArchiText*™, a program which can be used for content analysis on the Macintosh series of computers, lets the researcher construct a visual map of the abstractions and then link them to specific communications. In the left column are references to articles (called "nodes" in *ArchiText**) from the microcomputer news magazine *MacWeek*™, and on the right side is a visual abstraction of how one individual might organize these articles. In Figure 6.24, the nodes are linked to their specific mode of communication, in this case the magazine articles. *ArchiText* is unique in that it lets the researcher create a number of levels of abstraction to reduce communication to units which lend themselves to study and analysis.

## SUMMARY

In this chapter we have demonstrated the use of the microcomputer to help visualize data so that more sophisticated statistical techniques can be applied. Microcomputers can perform virtually every

---

*A node can be used for some other analysis unit besides an article.

FIGURE 6.24. Linking Actual Text to "Nodes" in *ArchiText* 1.0

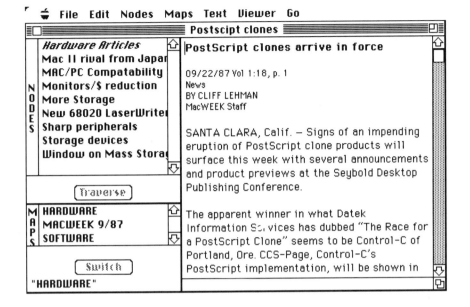

Text-Analysis Packages

| Apple Family | Apple Macintosh | IBM PC |
|---|---|---|
| Content Analysis National Collegiate Software Clearinghouse Duke University Press 6697 College Station Durham, NC 27708 (919)737-3067 | ArchiText BrainPower, Inc. 30497 Canwood St., Ste. 201 Agoura Hills, CA 91301 (800)345-0519 | Ethno National Collegiate Software Clearinghouse Duke University Press 6697 College Station Durham, NC 27708 (919)737-3067 |
| | Sonar Professional Virginia Systems Software Services, Inc. 5509 W. Bay Court Midlothian, VA 23112 (804)739-3200 | Ethnograph Qualis Research Associates P.O. Box 3785 Littleton, CO 80161 (303)795-6420 |

analysis now currently available on their mainframe counterparts. We illustrated examples of descriptive statistics, inferential statistics, and data-structure analyses, in addition to indicating how microcomputers might be applied to qualitative data.

# 7

# Disseminating the Results

## INTRODUCTION

We now come to the final steps in the research process: preparing reports, presentations, and press releases, and disseminating and helping others use the results. These steps are illustrated in Figure 7.1 and Table 7.1.

The real job of the researcher is not merely to do the research, but to communicate research results as widely as possible and in such a way that others can understand them. Yet dissemination— communication of the researcher's ideas (theories) and experimental results—often is taken for granted. Merely writing up results does not mean that anyone will find out about them or will find them interesting.

Having used the computer as a focus of integration, we now have a collection of proposals, data analysis, raw data, instruments, and drafts of results, all in electronic form. In this chapter we explore how to take this information and transform it into meaningful tables, figures, and even animate presentations. We discuss how to enhance the two traditional modes of communicating results—publishing articles in journals and giving oral presentations—and how to use a third mode: computer-conferencing systems.

Figure 7.2 shows how the computer can aid in dissemination. We discussed graphical analysis in Chapter 6. Since books present data in linear form, it is sometimes necessary to create artificial dichotomies for the sake of clear explanation. The reality is that creating graphics for presentation is very much like analysis. The goal of

## FIGURE 7.1.  Issues in Data Presentation and Dissemination

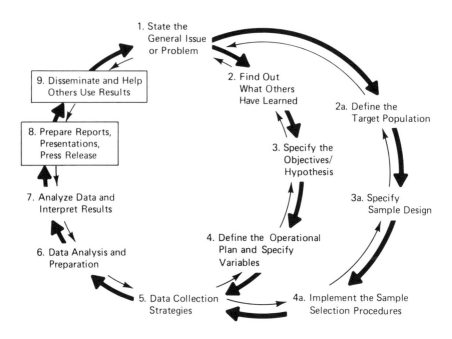

understanding our data and their possible results now becomes the goal of how best to communicate these to our intended audience.

Recall from Chapter 5 that we can capture data in a variety of ways. The preferable method is to gather the information electronically, since this reduces labor and increases accuracy. We discussed

## TABLE 7.1.    Research Matrix for Steps 8 and 9 on the Research Cycle

| Research Task | Application | Uses |
|---|---|---|
| **Step 8. Prepare Reports, Presentations, Press Releases** | | |
| Prepare Reports, Presentations, Press Releases, Display of Data | Word Processing Graphics Applications | Prepare Reports, Presentations, Press Releases, Display of Data |
| **Step 9. Disseminate and Help Others Use Results** | | |
| Disseminate and Help Others Use Results | Desktop Publishing, Bibliographic Reference Systems, Desktop Media, Presentation Software | Disseminate and Help Others Use Results |

FIGURE 7.2. Process of Computer-Aided Dissemination

| Data Preparation | Data Analysis | Graphic Enhancement | Presentation |
|---|---|---|---|
| Hand Coded | | Graphs | |
| | Exploratory Analysis | Computer Assisted | Written Report |
| Optically Scanned | Graphic Analysis | Drawing | |
| | | | Oral Presentations |
| Electronically Gathered | Statistical Analysis | Animated/Video Presentations | |

the statistical and exploratory analysis of data in Chapter 6. Once we have an understanding of what we believe our analysis is telling us, we can proceed to enhance our graphics to aid this understanding and to better communicate our findings. Ultimately, we will make an oral presentation or written report of our study and its findings. (Even if we will make an oral presentation, we normally begin by preparing it in written form.) Let's begin this chapter by returning to graphical analysis.

## GRAPHICAL ANALYSIS

The visual display of quantitative data is becoming increasingly popular (Tufte, 1983). To get a "feel" for their data, most analysts examine them in graphic form before using analytic techniques. Since it is easier to actually see relationships than to try to visualize them, the graphic presentation provides a means to ensure that the data meet the assumptions of the analytic technique (such as normality).

Returning to our earlier example of the *DARTS* game, consider the raw data from a set of trials given in Table 7.2. Given these data, the number crunchers among us (referred to as "data analysts" on our business cards) might jump right in and calculate a Pearson correlation. As demonstrated in Chapter 6, with a microcomputer we could calculate this correlation in the blink of an eye.

The Pearson *r* is a statistic that describes the linear relationship between two intervally scaled (and normally distributed) variables.* The *r* indicates two components of the bivariate relationship: degree

---

*Alternatively, we could use the regression coefficient if we were interested in examining an asymmetric relationship.

TABLE 7.2.    Hypothetical DART Data

| Number of Trials (X1) | Time Interval (Y1) |
|:---:|:---:|
| 2 | 4 |
| 2 | 6 |
| 2 | 5 |
| 4 | 7 |
| 4 | 10 |
| 4 | 10 |
| 6 | 13 |
| 6 | 14 |
| 6 | 15 |
| 8 | 16 |
| 8 | 17 |
| 8 | 21 |
| 10 | 18 |
| 10 | 19 |
| 10 | 20 |
| 12 | 19 |
| 12 | 20 |
| 12 | 21 |

and direction. The Pearson $r$ calculated by the computer for the two variables in Figure 7.2 is .88, which means that X1 (number of trials) and Y1 (time interval) have a strong, positive linear relationship to each other. Since students who are not so comfortable with numbers may have difficulty understanding (seeing) this relationship, it might be helpful to display the two variables graphically, as in Figure 7.3. The diagram was generated by the "scattergram" option in the Macintosh statistical analysis package, *Statview II*™:

Remember, these data have been "untouched by human hands." With almost no effort, we have transformed the data into graphic displays that help us understand and communicate results. We can point to our graph (we tell you in a later section how to display this) and show the audience how the variables are related: "When X1 increases, Y1 also increases."

Let's evaluate Figure 7.3 more closely. Data analysts know that the Pearson $r$ assumes linearity in the relationship between the two variables. This means that ideally the data should form a straight (linear) line. From a cursory inspection of our graph, they appear to do so. But in the upper right corner of the graph, where X1 and Y1

FIGURE 7.3. Graph of DART Data in *Statview II* (Macintosh)

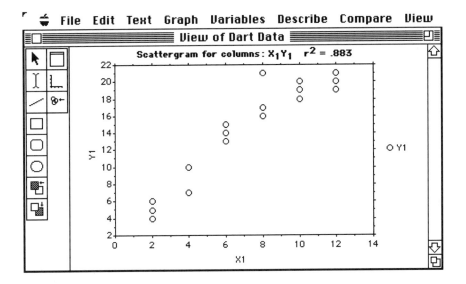

are largest, the relationship seems to curve a little. We can show the linearity of the relationship by regressing X1 on Y1. The regression will compute the linear equation between X1 and Y1. Figure 7.4 displays the *Statview II* results of this operation.

The straight line drawn through our graph represents a linear regression. The data seem to cluster very closely to this line but, just as we observed, those bothersome points in the upper right-hand portion of the plot appear to deviate (curve away) from the line. Hence, we are prompted to ask, is this a linear or curvilinear relationship? We could continue to investigate the problem with *Statview II* by choosing curvilinear regression analysis instead of linear. Instead, we have chosen to enhance our graph with software designed specifically for presentations.

*Cricket Graph*™ is a Macintosh display package that enables the user to make over 20 kinds of graphs, from simple line graphs to polar coordinate graphs. *Cricket Graph* can import data files created by Macintosh statistical analysis packages, such as *Systat, StatView II*, and others. Data also can be imported from other sources, such as spreadsheets or database packages. In our demonstration, we imported data into *Cricket Graph* from the *StatView II* analysis package by electronically "cutting and pasting"—pointing to our data, deleting or copying, opening up a *Cricket Graph* data window, and insert-

FIGURE 7.4. Regression Line for DART Data in *Statview II*

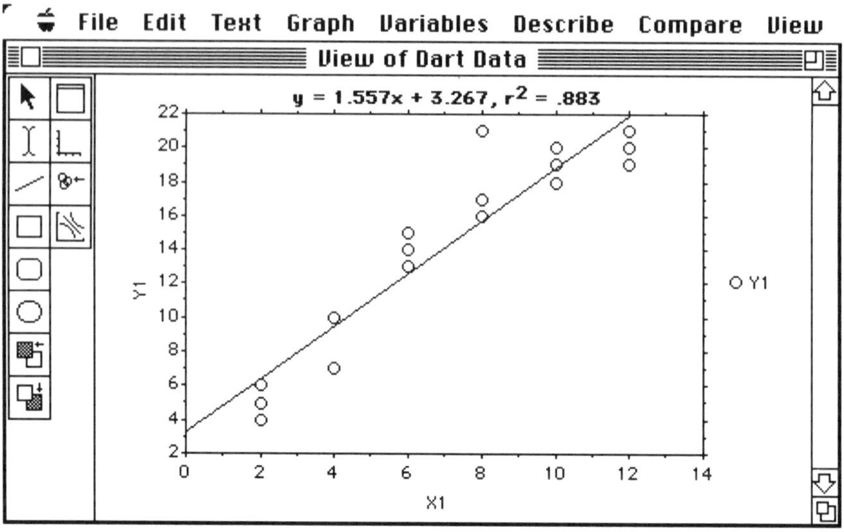

ing the data. This is only one of several ways to import data. The important thing is that we did not have to re-enter our data to use the *Cricket Graph* package.

*Cricket Graph* has a number of useful features, including labeling, color graph support, plotter support, curve fitting, and more. It can produce an attractive overhead transparency or slide as well. But let's return to the illustration of our curvilinear relationship.

An interesting phenomenon in the software industry is that many software applications began by emulating some manual function. For example, word-processing programs emulated typewriting, and graphics programs emulated charting. However, a trend we have observed is that software has begun to transcend simple emulation. *Cricket Graph* software can handle extremely complex statistical functions, and several statistics packages can produce some rather sophisticated charts.

We used *Cricket Graph* to regress our data by means of a polynomial model (third-order regression). How do we know it's a third-order equation? One way to find out is to just keep experimenting with equations of different orders until the best "fit" is obtained. The best "fit" generally is defined as that point at which deviations around the line are reduced to a minimum. Not too long ago, researchers were discouraged from exploring data-fitting steps because mainframe computer time was so expensive. The microcomputer has changed that. Because CPU time is essentially free (other than the cost of electricity), it encourages exploration. It is also a tremendous learning process. The value of exploration for a student is obvious, but this is not just for the student. Even the seasoned data analyst may wish to "play a few hunches" and explore the data.

The fit of the third-order regression is displayed in Figure 7.5. Note that *Cricket Graph* is capable of more sophisticated labelling than the graphics in the statistical-analysis package. Our graphic can now be imported into a word-processing package for inclusion in our written report.

All Macintosh word processors accept graphics, and many MS-DOS programs can now import graphics. *OS/2*™ and *Windows*™ are IBM-compatible operating systems designed to follow the conventions of the Macintosh, and the NeXt machine promises even more sophistication.

We may decide to print the graphic and also create a transparency or slide. This software can make a nice color plot and can even

FIGURE 7.5. Curvilinear Analysis Obtained by *Cricket Graph*

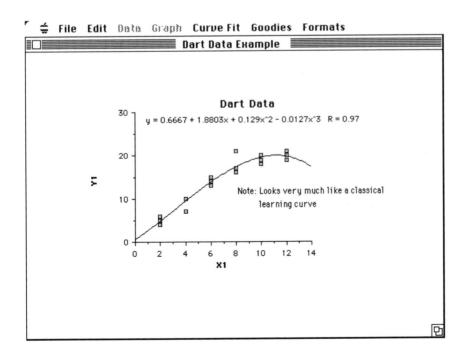

## Charting/Plotting Software

| Apple Family | Apple Macintosh | IBM PC |
|---|---|---|
| Graphics Department<br>Sensible Software, Inc.<br>335 E. Big Beaver, Ste. 207<br>Troy, MI 48083<br>(313)528-1950 | Cricket Graph<br>Cricket Software<br>40 Valley Stream Pkwy.<br>Malvern, PA 19355<br>(215)251-9890 | Graph-in-the-Box<br>New England Software, Inc.<br>Greenwich Office Park 3<br>Greenwich, CT 06831<br>(203)625-0062 |
| Ultra Plot<br>Abracadata Ltd.<br>P.O. Box 2440<br>Eugene, OR 97402<br>(503)342-3030 | Pixie Macintosh Version<br>Zenographics, Inc.<br>19752 MacArthur Blvd.<br>#220<br>Irvine, CA 92715<br>(714)851-6352 | Pixie<br>Zenographics, Inc.<br>19752 MacArthur Blvd.<br>#220<br>Irvine, CA 92715<br>(714)851-6352 |
| Data Ploting Software for<br>Micros 302<br>Kern International<br>100 Weymouth St., Ste. G1<br>Rockland, MA 02370<br>(717)871-4982 | Delta Graph<br>DeltaPoint<br>200 Heritage Harbor, Ste. G<br>Monterey, CA 93940<br>(800)873-0008 | Chart Master<br>Ashton-Tate<br>20101 Hamilton Ave.<br>Torrance, CA 90502-1319<br>(213)329-8000 |
| Scientific Plotter/<br>Curve Fitter<br>Compuware<br>15 Center Rd.<br>Randolph, NJ 07869<br>(201)366-8540 | TS Graph<br>Trimbur Software<br>Baka Industries<br>200 Pleasant Grove Rd.<br>Ithaca, NY 14850<br>(800)328-2252 | Lotus Graphwriter<br>Lotus Development Corp.<br>55 Cambridge Pkwy.<br>Cambridge, MA 02142<br>(617)577-8500 |
| PFS-Graph<br>Software Publishing Corp.<br>1901 Landings Dr.<br>Mountain View, CA 94043<br>(415)962-8910 | KaleidaGraph<br>Synergy Software (PCS, Inc.)<br>2457 Perkiomen Ave.<br>Reading, PA 19606<br>(215)779-0522 | Graph Master<br>Bridget Software Co.<br>1309 Canyon Rd.<br>Silver Spring, MD 20904<br>(301)384-7875 |

plot directly on the transparency in color. Excellent high-resolution color slides can be created with special slide-printing hardware (we discuss presentation hardware in a later section of this chapter). We also have the option of bringing a computer (perhaps a laptop) to a presentation and generating the graphics "live." This would require an LCD plate or a video-projection system. The presentation of "live" data has a number of advantages. The user can create graphics in response to the audience's questions, or lead the audience through the process step by step. The audience tends to develop rapport with the presenter, since the data are presented right before their eyes.

Often a researcher wants to create eye-catching visual displays to accompany a report. He or she may wish to create a higher quality report by exercising more control over the layout of text and graphics on a page than most word processors permit. Desktop-publishing software often is used for this purpose.


## DESKTOP PUBLISHING

The preparation of written reports has advanced in the past few years beyond the point of simply typing up results. Desktop publishing is a direct offshoot of technical microcomputer advances that integrate word-processing and graphic software with software for book and newspaper publishing. High-resolution laser printers use the same techniques found in very expensive typesetting systems to produce high-quality documents ready for publication.


### Document Processors

Many word processing programs have enough features to be quite useful as document processors, but the most sophisticated software programs are those specifically designed for desktop publishing. These packages integrate text, graphic, and even photographic information to give the operator total control over the layout of the page. For example, Figure 7.6 shows the screen of the popular Macintosh program, *PageMaker®*. (*PageMaker* is also available for accelerated MS-DOS machines, the IBM PS/2, and equivalent systems.)

*PageMaker* simulates the page-layout boards used in the publishing industry, on which objects such as pictures, graphs, or strips of text are literally cut and pasted. *PageMaker* performs all these functions electronically. It can do everything from automatically centering the title to determining page breaks. There are provisions for graphics, technical fonts, and special page layouts such as multicolumn displays.

Desktop-publishing systems give the researcher the capacity to closely match the publication quality of any journal. Many publishers are beginning to appreciate this "look Ma, no hands" technology and are accepting publication drafts mailed on floppy disk or transmitted via telecommunications (see Chapter 2). Today, most laser printers generate print at about 300 dpi (dots per inch), and more sophisticated printers capable of 1200 dpi are increasingly common.

FIGURE 7.6.  Screen from *PageMaker* 3.0,
a Desktop-Publishing Program

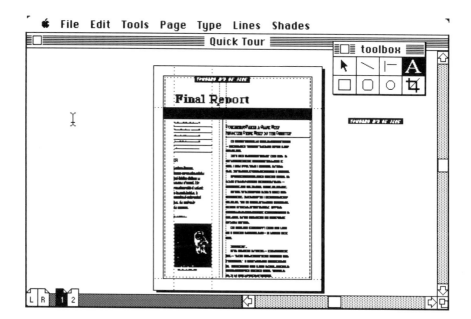

## Collections of Images

A number of software vendors have created image databases for desktop publishing, word processing, graphics, and other programs. Some large collections of images reside in CD-ROM for easy access and retrieval. The user need simply consult the database, select a picture that is relevant to the topic, and "cut and paste" the graphic into the document. For example, T/Maker Graphics has developed a series of art packages called *ClickArt®* for the Apple Macintosh. Figure 7.7 shows a map of the contiguous United States adapted from their "Publications" database. Normally it would take hours to create this map, but all we had to do was import the graphic and customize it for our purpose. It took roughly 15 minutes (and we're somewhat obsessive about detail). There are programs that can take demographic data entered by the user and display the information as crosshatches right on the map. *GeoQuery™*, a visual geographic analysis for the Macintosh computer, is an example.* *Systat* has this capacity, but

*Odesta Corp., 4084 Commercial Ave., Northbrook, IL 60062. Phone: (312)498-5615

## Document/Desktop-Publishing Software

| Apple Family | Apple Macintosh | IBM PC |
|---|---|---|
| Geopublish for the Apple Berkeley Softworks 2150 Shattuck Ave., Penthouse Suite Berkeley, CA 94704 (800)443-0100 | Aldus PageMaker for the Macintosh Aldus Corp. 411 First Ave. S., Ste 200 Seattle, WA 98104 (206)622-5500 | Aldus PageMaker for the PC Aldus Corp. 411 First Ave. S., Ste 200 Seattle, WA 98104 (206)622-5500 |
| GraphicWriter Seven Hills Software Corp. 2310 Oxford Rd. Tallahassee, FL 32304 (904)575-0566 | QuarkXPress Quark, Inc. 300 S. Jackson St., Ste. 100 Denver, CO 80209 (800)356-9363 | QuarkXPress Quark, Inc. 300 S. Jackson St., Ste. 100 Denver, CO 80209 (800)356-9363 |
| Publish-It! Timeworks, Inc. 444 Lake Cook Rd. Deerfield, IL 60015 (800)535-9497 | Publish-It! Timeworks, Inc. 444 Lake Cook Rd. Deerfield, IL 60015 (800)535-9497 | Publish-It! Timeworks, Inc. 444 Lake Cook Rd. Deerfield, IL 60015 (800)535-9497 |
| Springboard Publisher Springboard Software, Inc. 7808 Creekridge Cir. Minneapolis, MN 55435 (612)944-3915 | Ragtime 2 Cricket Software 40 Valley Stream Pkwy. Malvern, PA 19355 (215)251-9890 | IBM Interleaf Publisher Interleaf, Inc. 10 Canal Park Cambridge, MA 02141 (617)577-9800 |
| Printrix Data Transforms, Inc. 616 Washington St. Denver, CO 80203 (303)832-1501 | ReadySetGo! Letraset USA 40 Eisenhower Dr. Paramus, NJ 07653 (800)845-6100 | Xerox Ventura Publisher Xerox Desktop Software 9745 Business Park Dr. San Diego, CA 92131 (800)822-8221 |

generates its maps from a data file containing coordinates rather than from a graphic.

## GRAPHICS PROGRAMS

### Drawing Programs

In contrast to specialized graphic databases are programs that allow the researcher to create drawings "from scratch." For example, we imported the map in Figure 7.7 from the database, then en-

FIGURE 7.7.  Map of the United States from *ClickArt*

## Image Collections/Databases

| Apple Family | Apple Macintosh | IBM PC |
|---|---|---|
| Print Shop Graphics Library Broderbund Software, Inc. 17 Paul Dr. San Rafael, CA 94903-2101 (415)492-3200 | ClickArt Series T/Maker Co. 1390 Villa St. Mountain View, CA 94041 (415)962-0195 | Print Shop Graphics Library Broderbund Software, Inc. 17 Paul Dr. San Rafael, CA 94903-2101 (415)492-3200 |
| Graph Art Sensible Software, Inc. 335 E. Big Beaver, Ste. 207 Troy, MI 48083 (313)528-1950 | Cliptures/MacGallery Dream Maker Software 4020 Paige St. Los Angeles, CA 90031 (800)876-5665 | Cliptures Dream Maker Software 4020 Paige St. Los Angeles, CA 90031 (800)876-5665 |
| Clip Art Collection Works of Art Series Springboard Software, Inc. 7808 Creekridge Cir. Minneapolis, MN 55435 (612)944-3915 | Works of Art Springboard Software, Inc. 7808 Creekridge Cir. Minneapolis, MN 55435 (612)944-3915 | Clip Art Collection Springboard Software, Inc. 7808 Creekridge Cir. Minneapolis, MN 55435 (612)944-3915 |
| Art Gallery I/II/Fantasy Unison World 1321 Harbor Bay Pkwy. Alameda, CA 94501 (415)748-6670 | Adobe Collector's Editions Adobe Systems 1585 Charleston Rd., Box 7900 Mountain View, CA 94039 (800)344-8335 | Desktop Art Series Dynamic Graphics, Inc. 6000 N. Forest Park Dr. P.O. Box 1901 Peoria, IL 61656-1901 |

hanced the drawing by adding some text and lines showing where we live. Figure 7.8 is a picture created completely with *MacDraw II*®, a graphics program for the Apple Macintosh. This figure re-creates a screen very similar to the one displayed to students in the *DARTS* experiment. It conveys more clearly the nature of the task the subjects were asked to complete. We can make the graphic into a transparency to show to the audience during an oral presentation, or place it in a written report to further explain our experiment.

Drawing programs treat all images on the screen as objects. For example, in Figure 7.8 we used the mouse as a pen to draw straight lines to represent the wall and floor, a square to create the box representing Jack, and an ellipse to create the balloon. We used the "fill-in" function to give the balloon a pattern, and fonts to add text to the objects. Many programs can create images in color, and some support plotters.

FIGURE 7.8. DARTS Screen Created in *MacDraw II* (Macintosh)

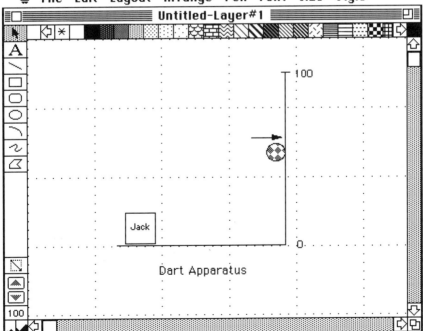

## Painting Programs

Unlike drawing programs, painting programs operate by generating pixels. *Pixel* is one of the cuter terms the computer world has cooked up and requires a little (some pun intended) explanation. Figure 7.9 illustrates the letter "A" magnified 1000% over its normal printed size. Notice that, upon magnification, what appears as a smooth, continuous line is really a series of black or white squares. Each square is called a pixel. The computer user can manipulate multiple pixels through the use of painting tools such as "spray cans," "brushes," and "pencils." For example, when a user types a letter, the program merely fills in the standard pixel pattern. However, most paint software allows the user to adjust the pattern at the pixel level, providing fine control over the apperance of final product. Paint software is more difficult and time-consuming than draw programs, but offers more control over detail.

One vital feature of painting and drawing programs is the ability to "undo" the last action or command. "Undoing" allows the budding computer artist to explore different alternatives or approaches without penalty. If the artist doesn't like what is created, he or she can revert the graphic back to the form it had before the last action

FIGURE 7.9.  Illustration of Pixels Forming the Letter "A"

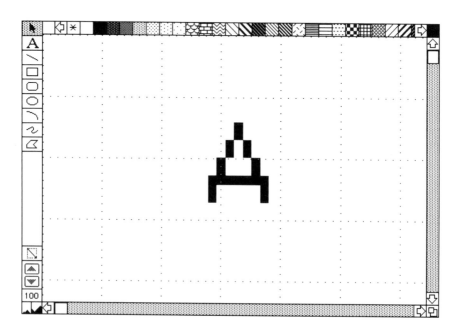

## Graphics Software

| Apple Family | Apple Macintosh | IBM PC |
|---|---|---|
| Paint<br>Baudville<br>5380 52nd St. S.E.<br>Grand Rapids, MI 59508<br>(616)698-0888 | SuperPaint<br>Silicon Beach Software<br>P.O. Box 261430<br>San Diego, CA 92126<br>(619)695-6956 | Draw Applause<br>Ashton-Tate<br>20101 Hamilton Ave.<br>Torrance, CA 90502<br>(213)329-8000 |
| Graphics Master<br>Sourceview Software Int'l<br>P.O. Box 578<br>Concord, CA 94522-0578<br>(415)686-8439 | FullPaint<br>Ashton-Tate<br>20101 Hamilton Ave.<br>Torrance, CA 90502<br>(213)329-8000 | PC Paintbrush<br>Publisher's Paintbrush<br>Zsoft Corp.<br>450 Franklin Rd., Ste. 100<br>Marietta, GA 30067<br>(404)428-0008 |
| Dazzle Draw<br>Broderbund Software, Inc.<br>17 Paul Dr.<br>San Rafael, CA 94903-2101<br>(415)492-3200 | MacDraw II<br>Claris Corp.<br>5201 Patrick Henry Dr.<br>P.O. Box 58168<br>Santa Clara, CA 95052<br>(800)544-8554 | Deluxepaint II<br>Electronic Arts<br>1820 Gateway Dr.<br>San Mateo, CA 94404<br>(415)571-7171 |
| Topdraw<br>Styleware, Inc.<br>440 Clyde Ave.<br>Mountain View, CA 94043<br>(415)960-1500 | Aldus FreeHand<br>Aldus Corp.<br>411 First Ave. S., Ste. 200<br>Seattle, WA 98104<br>(206)622-5500 | VP-Graphics<br>Paperback Software Int'l<br>2830 Ninth St.<br>Berkeley, CA 94710<br>(415)644-2116 |
| Graphic Edge<br>Pinpoint Publishing<br>5865 Doyle, Ste. 112<br>Emeryville, CA 94608<br>(415)654-3050 | PixelPaint<br>SuperMac Technology<br>485 Potrero Ave.<br>Sunnyvale, CA 94086<br>(408)245-2202 | Energraphics<br>Enertronics Research, Inc.<br>#5 Station Plaza<br>1910 Pine St.<br>St. Louis, MO 63103<br>(314)421-2771 |

or command. Another important feature is the ability to delete objects or pixels on the screen, or cut and paste images into the same or other graphic pictures. One package, *SuperPaint*™ (for the Macintosh), combines most of the features of both paint and draw programs.

### Scanners

The scanner is a fascinating and useful tool. In Chapter 6 we mentioned the use of optical scanners to input data such as test results or data from survey questionnaires. A scanner can also be used to reproduce graphic information. In this mode, it operates much like a copy machine, except that it stores the image in electronic form so that it can be imported (pasted) into a graphic or document. Advanced scanners can produce very sharp images similar in quality to those in a good newspaper. This unlocks limitless possibilities for graphs and pictures in presentations and papers. The researcher is no longer text-bound.

We have hypothesized that the reason text predominates in books and journal articles is that the typewriter and the printing press created an easy means to generate text-based documents. In the future we think that text will be supplemented by graphics as a means of communicating research results.

Ironically, advances in the computer may well take us back to a time in which we can communicate with both words and pictures, and with greater ease than with paper-based technology. The modern microcomputer will enhance communication by its ability to store, retrieve, and support words, pictures, video, and sound (i.e., multimedia).

## OTHER FORMS OF DISSEMINATION

### Presentation Software

Imagine presenting your results by taking your audience through a three-dimensional representation of the data. Imagine being able to link spectacular sound and video images to your presentation. Just a few years ago this feat would have required a million-dollar setup, such as those available only to major television studios. Now just about anyone with advanced microcomputer literacy can have access to all of these marvelous tools for about $10,000. And that figure keeps going down, while at the same time ease of use keeps improving. Figure 7.10 shows one "slide" in an animated sequence produced with the presentation software package *VideoWorks*™.*

In our *DARTS* experiment, we might be interested in demonstrating to our audience just how screen interaction took place for a given student or class of students, that is, how the coordinates were input and how the darts were thrown. We might re-create this as an animation sequence in *VideoWorks*. Alternatively, *VideoWorks* could

---

*Spinnaker Software, 201 Broadway, Cambridge, MA 02139. Phone: (617)494-1200

FIGURE 7.10. *VideoWorks* Production Screen (Macintosh)

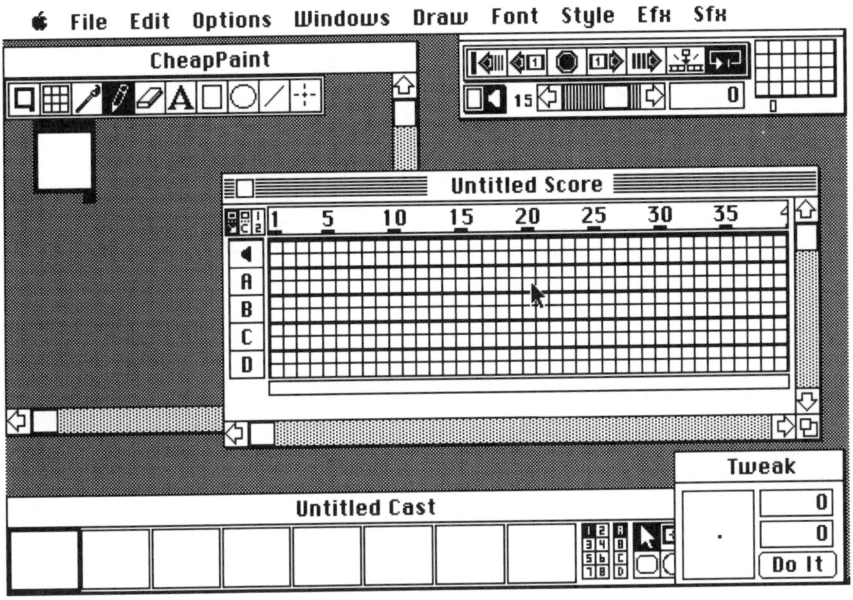

be used to show subjects what they are supposed to do during, or even before, the experimental trials.

## Presentation Managers

Presentation managers are useful for organizing graphic and text presentations. They can be used to organize and print transparencies or slides to present the same information "live."

*Slide Show Magician*™ is an Apple Macintosh software program that allows the researcher to take a "string" of images created by drawing programs and assemble them for a set presentation.* It enables the user to change the sequence of images and to present them in a controlled mode, such as a slide projector, or in a timed mode, wherein each individual graphic (slide) is displayed for a prescribed time before the next one appears. Similar programs are available for

*Magnum Software, 21115 Devonshire St., Ste. 337, Chatsworth, CA 91311.
  Phone: (818)700-0510

## Presentation Software

| Apple Family | Apple Macintosh | IBM PC |
|---|---|---|
| Frame-Up<br>Beagle Brothers<br>6215 Serris Sq., Ste. 100<br>San Diego, CA 92121<br>(800)345-1750<br>(800)992-4022 in CA | Microsoft PowerPoint<br>Microsoft Corporation<br>16011 NE 36th Way<br>Box 97017<br>Redmond, WA 98073<br>(800)426-9400 | Microsoft PowerPoint<br>Microsoft Corporation<br>16011 NE 36th Way<br>Box 97017<br>Redmond, WA 98073<br>(800)426-9400 |
| The Slide Projector<br>Conduit<br>University of Iowa<br>Oakdale Campus<br>Iowa City, IA 52242<br>(319)335-4100 | Aldus Persuasion<br>Aldus Corp.<br>411 First Ave. S., Ste. 200<br>Seattle, WA 98104<br>(206)622-5500 | Harvard Presentation<br>Graphics<br>Software Publishing Corp.<br>1901 Landings Dr.<br>Mountain View, CA 94043<br>(415)962-8910 |
| Showoff<br>Broderbund Software, Inc.<br>17 Paul Dr.<br>San Rafael, CA 94903-2101<br>(415)492-3200 | Cricket Presents<br>Cricket Software<br>40 Valley Stream Pkwy.<br>Malvern, PA 19355<br>(215)251-9890 | Pyxel Visuals<br>Pyxel Applications, Inc.<br>P.O. Box 35971<br>Richmond, VA 23235<br>(804)320-5573 |
|  | StandOut!<br>Letraset USA<br>40 Eisenhower Dr.<br>Paramus, NJ 07653<br>(800)845-6100 | Present-It<br>Power Up Software Corp.<br>2929 Campus Dr., Ste. 400<br>P.O. Box 7600<br>San Mateo, CA 94403<br>(415)345-5900 |

the IBM and Apple II products. Although they have been used very little by the general public, they are innovative ways of organizing lectures and presentations in business or education.

One of the most impressive and promising presentation managers is *HyperCard*. Not long ago, a *Hypercard* "stack" was effectively used by the Secretary of the Interior at a Congressional subcommittee hearing. In response to questions, the Secretary could instantly retrieve charts, graphs, and tables of information simply by pointing to a computer screen. The reaction of Congress to this presentation was overwhelmingly positive. Never before had a presentation been given wherein all of the facts and charts could be recalled as fast as the Secretary could explain them.

The advantage of a presentation manager such as *HyperCard* is its ability to link information (graphs, pictures, or text) in a nonlinear way. Retrieval is done simply by pointing at the linkages (repre-

FIGURE 7.11.  Opening Screen of *HyperCard* 1.2.5 Hypermedia
              Software (Macintosh)

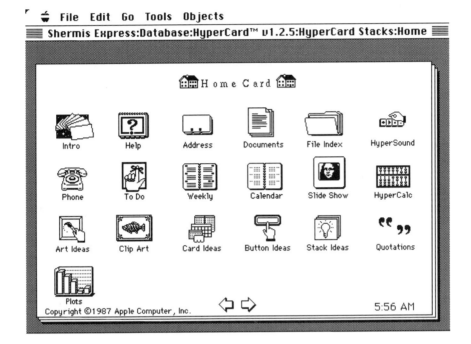

## Hypermedia Software

| Apple Family | Apple Macintosh | IBM PC |
|---|---|---|
| Hyperstudio<br>Roger Wagner<br>Publishing, Inc.<br>1050 Pioneer Way, Ste. P<br>El Cajon, CA 92020<br>(619)442-0522 | HyperCard<br>Apple Computer, Inc.<br>20525 Mariani Ave.<br>Cupertino, CA 95014<br>(408)996-1010 | LinkWay<br>IBM Corp./Applications<br>Systems Division<br>472 Wheeler Farms Rd.<br>Milford, CT 06460<br>(203)783-7000 |
| | SuperCard<br>Silicon Beach Software<br>P.O. Box 261430<br>San Diego, CA 92126<br>(619)695-6956 | Guide<br>Owl International, Inc.<br>2800 156th S.E.<br>Bellevue, WA 98007<br>(800)34-HYPER |

sented by "buttons") on a screen and clicking a computer mouse. Packages using hypermedia in this way are available for IBM-compatible computers; *LinkWay*™ is one such product. Figure 7.11 illustrates *HyperCard*'s "Home" stack card.

## PROJECTION SYSTEM HARDWARE

A video-projection system displays on a large screen what users see on their computer screen. Using "live" computer images makes for an effective presentation. In some ways, that makes it a rather risky business (we learned the hard way always to have backup transparencies!), but we've found that the rewards far outweigh the risks.

Many factors must be considered in using projection systems: the type of computer and the type of video output, the type of projection system and the type of input it accepts, and the type of software the user selects. Most projection systems, except for the very, very expensive ones (i.e., $40,000+), do not give as crisp a picture as an overhead transparency or slide. Some of the older models (over five years old) require the audience to sit in a dark room. However, within the next five years or so we anticipate that projection systems that handle microcomputer output will be as common as overhead projectors are today, and will have the same quality and resolution.

Most computers supply a "video out" source which can be attached to the "video input" on the projector; or, with the aid of a skilled technician, they can be so configured. Anyone considering a projection system will need to be familiar with a number of technical factors:

1. What scan rates will the projector be required to handle? The scan rate is the speed at which the computer screen is repainted. Scan rates for most computers range from 5–30 MHz. These figures usually are published in the product specifications.

2. Will there be a need to project color? Displays can be enhanced by color, and most computers can project some form of color. Video output usually comes in two forms: "line" or NTSB (National Television Standard Band) and RGB (Red, Green, and Blue). The user will need to know which type the computer displays.]

3. Will graphics be displayed? A number of projectors can display text, but do not have the resolution to show graphics.

Administrative factors, such as anticipated size of audience, portability, and cost, will be just as important.

At present, video-projection systems are of two types. One projects a color image in much the same way as a television monitor. The other uses a Liquid Crystal Display (LCD), a piece of transparent glass through which the video output from the computer screen passes, creating an image as on a transparency. The LCD slate is placed on the overhead just like a transparency, and the presentation software (or any other program, e.g., a statistics package) changes the images on the screen. However, LCD displays do not project color very well (although this is beginning to change), and do not yet do a very good job of projecting sharp graphic images.

## INTEGRATED PACKAGES

Integration has been an important theme throughout this book. Word processing, database management, graphic presentations, telecommunications and networking, spreadsheets, and statistical programs all provide the researcher with a variety of useful tools. But there is one problem. Each program has its own unique command structure and stores and retrieves data in specific and unique ways, leading to incompatibility among programs and making the data difficult to import and export. Recognizing this problem, the software industry has offered a solution: integrated software packages that combine several applications under one general program. Combinations typically include word processor, spreadsheet, database manager, and telecommunications modules. A drawing or graphics program may also be incorporated.

This approach has two distinct advantages over one-application packages: the data share a common form and therefore can be used in many different applications, and the user need learn only one set of command procedures, which cuts down on learning time and prevents confusion.

All the major developers are taking steps to help integrate various types of software. The Macintosh operating system offers the ability to integrate software so that all packages share the same command and data structures. The same is true for the *Windows* operating system developed by the Microsoft Corporation. An interesting feature of the command structure of both operating systems is the use of a computer mouse or other input device (e.g., a touch screen) to accomplish system tasks by pointing to commands and options and to obtain help. When users become oriented to this pointing system, they feel comfortable running just about any software.

## Popular Integrated Software

| Apple Family | Apple Macintosh | IBM PC |
|---|---|---|
| AppleWorks<br>Claris Corp.<br>5201 Patrick Henry Dr.<br>P.O. Box 58168<br>Santa Clara, CA 95052<br>(800)544-8554 | Microsoft Works<br>Microsoft Corporation<br>16011 NE 36th Way<br>Box 97017<br>Redmond, WA 98073<br>(800)426-9400 | Microsoft Works<br>Microsoft Corporation<br>16011 NE 36th Way<br>Box 97017<br>Redmond, WA 98073<br>(800)426-9400 |
| Do-Re-Me<br>Multisoft<br>120 E. 90th St., Box 5J<br>New York, NY 10128<br>(212)534-4047 | Executive Office/My Office<br>DataPak Software<br>14011 Ventura Blvd.,<br>Ste. 507<br>Sherman Oaks, CA 91423<br>(818)905-6419 | Enable<br>Enable Software Inc.<br>Northway 10 Executive Park<br>Ballston Lake, NY 12019<br>(800)888-0684 |
| Magic Office System<br>ArtSci, Inc.<br>P.O. Box 1848<br>Burbank, CA 91505<br>(818)843-4080 | ProDesk<br>Mission Accomplished<br>Software Services, Inc.<br>10615 Bradbury Rd.<br>Los Angeles, CA 90064<br>(213)870-2441 | Symphony<br>Lotus Development Corp.<br>55 Cambridge Parkway<br>Cambridge, MA 02142<br>(617)577-8500 |
| VIP Professional<br>ISD Marketing, Inc.<br>2651 John St., Ste. 3<br>Markham, Ontario L3R 2W5<br>Canada<br>(416)479-1991 | | Framework III<br>Ashton-Tate<br>20101 Hamilton Ave.<br>Torrance, CA 90502<br>(213)329-8000 |

Integrated packages can be especially helpful to the beginner, and may be useful to the researcher who wishes to integrate his or her own computer-assisted work. The only drawback of many of these packages is that they may not offer all the features of stand-alone packages.

## COMPUTER CONFERENCES, BULLETIN BOARDS, AND FORUMS

We mentioned computer conferences and other telecommunications systems in Chapter 2, in our discussion of how to find out what others know. We have now come full circle. Now that we know something, and think we have some eloquent ways of sharing it, we are ready to sign onto these networks and tell our fellow researchers all about it.

## SUMMARY

A study is not complete until the results are summarized and disseminated. There are many vehicles for disseminating information via computers. We can use desktop publishing to make our printed reports look professional and attractive, and enhance them through graphics creation, retrieval, and manipulation. But the printed word is only one avenue for telling others what we have learned. Presentation programs can make our oral reports interesting and entertaining. Presentation software can utilize the older slide-and-transparency technology or permit you to give a "live" report. The advantage of being able to create and display information "on the fly" is that you can adapt your report to the needs of your audience. This presentation style is foreign to many of us but, once learned, can produce quite gratifying results. Integrated and hypermedia software hold the promise of being able to manage different aspects of the dissemination process in one package. Finally, telecommunications links are perhaps one of the fastest ways to communicate results to a select audience of colleagues or clients.

Up to now we have presented a relatively logical (we hope) description of how computers can be integrated with research. But just as research doesn't always turn out the way we planned, neither does the application of computer technology to research. In the final chapter we examine some of the perils, pitfalls, and promises of using microcomputers in social science research.

# 8

# Perils, Pitfalls, and Promises

*"The classifications of the constituents of a chaos, nothing else here is essayed...."*

—HERMAN MELVILLE, *Moby Dick*

## INTRODUCTION

Throughout this book we have sung the praises of the microcomputer as the Swiss-Army-knife equivalent of a research tool. While we haven't spoken much about the cost of using the microcomputer, the price of the computer hardware probably will be only about a fourth of your total investment in this technology. Most of your money will go toward the purchase of software, software upgrades, and media. Software is becoming more and more affordable and many large organizations can purchase a site license which permits making multiple copies, usually at a reduced price. Other discounts are available to educational organizations.

Our own personal experience is that you probably won't end up saving money using microcomputer technology, but rather will find yourself using the microcomputer for additional applications. In any event, your use of the microcomputer almost certainly will improve your work and allow you to do more of it, or the same amount in less time.

Where appropriate, we have cautioned you about particular software applications. However, as with most books, we have talked more about the positive than the negative side of our subject. Still, we did not feel we should coax you to enter Wonderland without at least a few words of warning about the Mad Hatter. So following are a few words on the perils, pitfalls, and promises of computer-based research.

## THE REALITY OF THE RESEARCH CYCLE

In reality, the research cycle looks more like the diagram in Figure 8.1. However, we didn't want to scare you off first thing, nor could we have explained it to you adequately. But our diagram of the somewhat chaotic nature of research (cf. Gleick, 1987) proves our point about computers even better: The microcomputer brings some order out of the chaos. If, on the other hand, one believes that research is an orderly process (Kuhn, 1970), even so, using the microcomputer promotes and encourages further structure. In our research, we've been saved by the computer more than once when we failed to find a printed copy of an article or reference, yet were able to retrieve it electronically from the computer. We also lost countless hours of

FIGURE 8.1. The Chaotic Nature of the Reseach Cycle

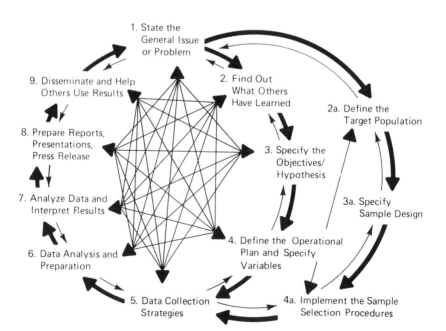

work more than once as victims of one of the perils we describe below. There were some agonizing moments when we felt the computer was winning the battle *against* our getting research done. But there were many moments of triumph when we knew we'd saved countless hours and produced work better than anything we'd done before, thanks to the microcomputer.

## THE PERILS

*"Cap'n, the dilithium crystals can't take much more of this. She's gonna blow!"*
—ENGINEER SCOTT TO CAPTAIN KIRK, *Star Trek*

Even 21st-century machines have their limitations. Listed in Table 8.1 and described below are some of the perils of microcomputer technology; no doubt there are others.

**TABLE 8.1.    Perils of Computer-based Research**

| The Peril | Definition |
|---|---|
| The Power Failure Fiasco | Sudden loss of power (or brown-out) resulting in loss of all work currently on the system. This usually happens when you work for several hours on a document and forget to save it every few minutes. |
| Disk Devils | $5\frac{1}{4}''$ disks come in the following memory sizes; 140K, 360K, 1.2 Meg. $3\frac{1}{2}''$ disks come in 400K, 720K, 800K, 1.4 Meg, 2.8 Meg. Most of these formats are on different machines, and many are incompatible with each other. |
| Double Indemnity | Although great advances in software and hardware have been made, when the computer is being used for the first time, it never hurts to double the time estimate for finishing a job. |
| Hardware Dependency | It never fails that it fails some time. When you are about to make the presentation of your life, that's when you are liable to experience a hardware failure. |
| The Hal 2000 Principle | As the software gets easier to use, it gets more complex; and the more complex it gets, the more likely it is to have a bug. The most insidious bug is the one that waits for just that unusual combination of computer events, then bam!—corruption. And the worst part is, when you show your best friend, it works fine. |

### The Power Failure Fiasco

Each of us can tell you a story, or knows of someone else's story, about power failure. Like many an undergraduate scholar, Paul used to wait until the last minute to do term papers on his typewriter. The paper had to be perfect in its first draft, since there was no time for editing. One night, while practicing the same philosophy in graduate school (this time using a microcomputer and word-processing software), Paul finished a 20-page paper, rose to turn on the printer, and accidentally kicked his computer's power plug out of the electrical socket. Of course he hadn't saved a word of his document onto a floppy or hard disk, so he lost four hours of work and, even worse, his original design and thoughts. Unfortunately, Paul is a two-trial learner—it wasn't until after the second time he lost some important work that he learned to save information onto disk, and to save it often.

### Disk Devils

Disk Devils take many forms. The worst problem is the incompatibility between the $3\frac{1}{2}$- and $5\frac{1}{4}$-inch "standards." This problem, however, is gradually being solved. Telecommunications programs, for instance, can be used to transfer files from one machine to another by saving them as text files (with the loss of formatting and fonts) and importing one into the other. They also can be transfered by uploading to a mainframe or minicomputer and then downloading to another machine.

Sometimes we may want to give someone a file in which one person used *Wordstar 2000*™ and another *WordPerfect*™.* Many software packages have built-in "translators" so that they can read both data and formatting indicators of other packages. For example, *WordPerfect* can read a file created by *Wordstar 2000* and keep all formatting intact. Also, specialized translators such as *MacLink Plus*™ can transfer information from MS-DOS machines to Macintosh computers, and vice versa.† The Apple Macintosh can now read and even format MS-DOS diskettes ($3\frac{1}{2}$″ floppies). It appears that in the future most machines will use some form of a standard operating system, such as UNIX. Such systems eventually may lead to the standardization that the microcomputer industry (or at least the user) desperately needs.

---

* *Wordstar 2000* is developed by Micropro International Corp., 33 San Pablo Ave., San Rafael, CA 94903, Phone: (800)227-5609; *WordPerfect* is developed by WordPerfect Corp., 1555 N. Technology Way, Orem, UT 04057, Phone: (801)225-5000

† Datavisz, Inc., 35 Corporate Dr., Trumbull, CT 06611. Phone: (203)268-0030

Other insidious problems can emanate from the disk or the drive itself. Recently we had a disk drive fail in such a way that it ruined whatever disk was placed in the drive. Or sometimes the disk itself will fail. Such failures can happen quite unexpectedly. Disaster is best avoided by making backup copies of the files on different disks and keeping them in different places. Fortunately, disk problems happen very infrequently; the reliability of hardware and disks usually is quite good.

### Double Indemnity

Just as we begin to feel confident in our ability to use these systems, someone asks for help. Sometimes they ask us to help set up a database or spreadsheet. At other times they ask us to help set up a computer-assisted data-collection system. Our rule of thumb, from experience, is to estimate the time it will take to complete the task and multiply by two.

Double indemnity does not hold for word processing (by an experienced user), using a spreadsheet for budgets, or similar routine jobs. The more we gain experience with these systems, the faster we become. Similarly, statistical tools (those that don't try to clone their mainframe big brothers) are much simpler and faster to use on the microcomputer.

### Hardware Dependency

Hardware systems are sufficiently complicated that sometimes one loose or out-of-place wire can cause the entire computer to fail. Sometimes problems can be quite deceptive. The only cure is to become very familiar with your computer system, or to make sure that when you are about to give the presentation of your life, someone with the necessary technical background is there to support you. In most education or business environments, in a pinch you usually can borrow a colleague's computer or LCD slate. It never hurts to have a source of backup hardware in mind. Having a backup presentation on transparencies or in printed form is also a prudent move.

### The Hal 2000 Principle

Sci Fi buffs will recognize Hal 2000 as the computer-gone-haywire in the movie *2001: A Space Odyssey*. We chose it as an apt illustration of how incredibly high levels of sophistication can lead to incredibly catastrophic problems—a variation on the "the bigger they are, the harder they fall" theory. For example, American Telephone and Telegraph (AT&T) has some of the most sophisticated computers and software in the world, yet one winter night their entire East Coast system overloaded due to a computer malfunction. Sometimes programmers will make additions to existing programs that have run well, but as they increase the complexity of the program, they increase the odds of the program making an error. Some programs may run error free tens of thousands of times, but then one special combination of conditions triggers an error. The only way to protect yourself against this peril is to save your work, and save it often.

## THE PITFALLS

The pitfalls we speak about here (summarized in Table 8.2) are those created by microcomputer technology itself. The way to avoid them is to be alert and wary.

### Information Overload

Information overload can result from the use of automated data-collection devices, since the computer can quickly collect more data than one can possibly analyze. Aggregating these data may be difficult, but is a necessary task. The same problem can occur when we retrieve hundreds of citations via automated retrieval programs. In some cases, only a computer can sort out what a computer has retrieved. The best way to avoid overload is to define the objectives (and limitations) of the study carefully, so that you don't collect extraneous information.

### If the Computer Says So. . . .

Just because you get an answer to a question from a computer doesn't automatically mean that it is correct. Today's computer software is designed to maximize "ease of use," which means that it can permit you to accomplish a task that under other circumstances would have been impossible or improbable. For example, many statistical-analysis packages permit you to perform an analysis of variance (ANOVA) on a nominally scaled dependent variable. While there are statistical techniques to address situations where the dependent

TABLE 8.2.   Pitfalls of Computer-based Research

| The Peril | Definition |
| --- | --- |
| Information Overload | Too much information for the senses to comprehend. |
| If the Computer Says So. . . . | A variant on the GIGO maxim: garbage in, garbage out. |
| Perfectionism | The ease of making changes in the document makes it hard to know when to stop. |
| Golly-gee-whiz-bang Graphics | Graphic presentations that distort the data or look more interesting than the data actually warrant. |
| Analysis Paralysis | The ease of generating statistical analysis makes it tempting to throw in every analysis possible (and the computer may even analyze the impossible). The result is similar to information overload, since the researcher may forget the original research question he or she sought to answer. |

variable is nominally scaled, ANOVA is not one of them, since one of the assumptions underlying ANOVA is that the dependent variable is at least intervally scaled. The program will still give you some output—it will just be wrong.

### Perfectionism

Some computer users become so mesmerized by the ease with which they can modify their documents that they lose track of the latest version of their work. Also, the ease at which revisions can be made seems to promote more stringent standards. Before the days of word processing, faculty often would pity their doctoral and master's students by withholding some of their more esoteric editing suggestions, since changing one page could mean retyping and renumbering the entire paper or thesis. Now professors don't hesitate to recommend changes. Students may find this a bit upsetting, but it probably improves their research reporting.

### Golly-gee-whiz-bang Graphics

The graphics packages illustrated in the previous chapter can make even random numbers look good. Surprisingly, a lot of people can be fooled by the appearance of professional-looking graphics that have little real meaning. One graphics trick made easier by the computer is simply changing the scale, which causes results to appear either larger or smaller. As with all uses of the microcomputer, to make intelligent charts the researcher must have a fundamental statistical base. Without it, the user simply produces professional-looking graphs that say nothing—or worse, say the wrong thing.

### Analysis Paralysis

This is the most interesting pitfall of computer-based research. Experienced researchers who are familiar with data analysis may escape becoming paralyzed by the computer's ability to print reams of statistics, but nevertheless can be dismayed at having to wade through pages of statistical nonsense looking for the specific analyses that answer their questions. The person who is just beginning to understand research usually is overwhelmed by all the numbers and may take days to go through the printouts. In the process, it is easy to lose sight of the original research question. In a previous chapter, we encouraged the user to explore. Now, mindful of this pitfall, we exhort the researcher to heed the fine line between intelligent exploration and a fishing expedition.

## THE PROMISES

The automation of machinery had a dramatic impact on the industrial revolution. According to Zuboff (1986), "informating" will have a similar effect on the information revolution. We believe we have shown that informating the research process can liberate the researcher to do what he or she does best: think. Zuboff has shown that informating can be a two-edged sword. Along with all of its benefits, it also has the power to amplify ignorance and to isolate and dehumanize people. We hope to be on the other cutting edge. We have shown that networks have the capacity to help people communicate more efficiently, quickly, and effectively. It is a wonderful experience to teach a class and watch as students share their bibliographic references and learn the power of working together.

Much of what we describe in this book has to do with ways to automate the research process. But in exploring the use of the computer to improve research, we are finding techniques that are unique in that they can be done only with a computer. Many people seek computer "cookbooks" that will tell them exactly how, what, and when to do something, but we have learned that such an approach stifles the creative uses of this powerful tool.

The common thread throughout this book has been to encourage our readers to manipulate information in an integrated fashion—to grab hold of it much like they would a gem, to hold it in their hands and examine it from all sides, then to take pictures of it and describe it to others. The computer allows us to explore information this thoroughly.

We view doing research as like making music. The computer is our instrument and we are the musicians. Sometimes we solo; sometimes our best work is in symphony. The computer puts fun, creativity, and excitement into the process while it takes the difficult labor out. The greatest promise of the technology is that anyone can master the instrument, so all of us can make beautiful music.

# References

Andrews, F. M., Klem, L., Davidson, T. N., O'Malley, P. M., & Rodgers, W. L. (1981). *A guide for selecting statistical techniques for analyzing social science data* (2nd ed.). Ann Arbor, MI: Institute for Social Research, The University of Michigan.

Assadi, B. (1989). Mac word processors: A blend of features. *InfoWorld, 11*(34), S1-S15.

Baker, J. G., & Whitehead, G. (1972). Technical note: A portable recording apparatus for rating behavior In free-operant situations. *Journal of Applied Behavior Analysis, 5,* 191-192.

Berger, C. F., Pintrich, P. R., & Stemmer, P. M. (1987). Cognitive consequences of student estimation on linear and logarithmic estimation. *Journal of Research in Science Teaching, 24*(5), 437-450.

Berger, C. F., Shermis, M. D., & Stemmer, P. M. (1982). *Data gathering, analysis, and display using microcomputers.* Training session given at the Annual Meetings of the American Educational Research Association, New York, NY.

Borenstein, M., & Cohen, J. (1988). *Statistical power analysis: A computer program.* Hillsdale, NJ: Lawrence Erlbaum Associates, Inc.

Borg, W. R., & Gall, M. D. (1989). *Educational research: An introduction* (5th ed.). New York: Longman.

Carpenter, J. D., & Morganstein, D. (1984). Statistical software for microcomputers. *Byte, 9*(4), 234-264.

Carr, J. J. (1980). *Microcomputer interfacing handbook: A/D & D/A.* Blue Ridge Summit, PA: Tab Books.

Chandler, L. A. (1983). The Stress Response Scale: An instrument for use in assessing emotional adjustment reactions. *School Psychology Review, 12,* 260-265.

Chandler, L. A. (1985). *The Children's Life Events Inventory: Instructions for use.* Unpublished mimeo. The Psychoeducational Clinic, University of Pittsburgh.

Cohen, J. (1988). *Statistical power analysis for the behavioral sciences* (2nd ed.). Hillsdale, NJ: Lawrence Erlbaum Associates, Inc..

Edelson, J. L. (1978). An inexpensive instrument for rapid recording of in vivo observations. *Journal of Applied Behavior Analysis, 11*(4), 502.

Fridlund, A. J. (1988). Statistics software. *InfoWorld, 10*, 55-76.

Gleick, J. (1987). *Chaos: Making a new science.* New York: Viking.

Groves, R. M., & Kahn, R. L. (1979). *Surveys by telephone: A national comparison with personal interviews.* New York: Academic Press.

Harshbarger, T. R. (1971). *Introductory statistics: A decision map.* New York: Macmillan.

Hussain, D., & Hussain, K. M. (1986). *The computer challenge: Technology, applications, and social implications.* Edina, MN: Burgess Communications.

Johnson, C. W. (1983). *Microcomputers in educational research* (TM 830 124). Princeton, NJ: ERIC Clearinghouse on Tests, Measurement, and Evaluation.

Jöreskog, K. G., & Sörbom, D. (1984). *LISREL VI: Analysis of linear structural relationships by maximum likelihood, instrumental variables, and least square methods.* Mooresville, IN: Scientific Software, Inc.

Kish, L. (1965). *Survey sampling.* New York: John Wiley.

Kuhn, T. S. (1962). *The structure of scientific revolutions.* Chicago: University of Chicago Press.

Lachenbruch, P. A. (1983). Statistical programs for microcomputers. *Byte, 8*(11), 560-570.

Lombardi, J. (1988). Word processing for professionals and offices. *InfoWorld, 10*(13), 53-72.

Madron, T. W., Tate, C. N., & Brookshire, R. G. (1985). *Using microcomputers in research.* Beverly Hills, CA: Sage Publications, Inc.

Meike, B. (1987). *MindLab.* Ventura, CA: Kinko's Academic Courseware Exchange.

Neffendorf, H. (l983). Statistical packages for microcomputers: A listing. *The American Statistician, 37*(1), 83-86.

Newman, R. F., & Berger, C. F. (1984). Children's estimation: Flexibility in the use of counting. *Journal of Child Psychology, 76*(1), 55-64.

Peterson, R. A., & Reiss, S. (1987). *Anxiety Sensitivity Index manual.* Palos Heights, IL: International Diagnostic Systems, Inc.

PSRC Software. (1986). *MaCATI.* Bowling Green, OH: Author.

Raskin, R. (1989). Testing for significance. *PC Magazine, 5*(5), 103-255.

Sculley, J. (1988). *Odyssey: Pepsi to Apple, a journey of adventure, ideas, and the future.* New York: Harper & Row.

Shermis, M. D. (1983). Calculating necessary sample sizes the easy way. [Review of SampleCalc]. *Contemporary Educational Review, 1*(4), 56-57.

Shermis, M. D. (1987). *The implementation of computer adaptive testing in a hypermedia environment.* Grant proposal funded by the University Research Institute, Austin, TX: The University of Texas at Austin.

Shermis, M. D., Cole, R., & Heyden, R. (1990). *HyperStat II*. Austin, TX: The University of Texas at Austin.

Shermis, M. D., & Givner, C. (1986). Implications of analog-to-digital technology for social sciences: A review and preview. *Social Science Microcomputer Review, 4*(3), 295-309.

StatSoft. (1985). *Q-fast: The complete computerized testing system*. Tulsa, OK: Author.

Stemmer, J. P. M., & Berger, C. B. (1985). *A guide to selecting microcomputer statistical packages*. Princeton, NJ: ERIC Tests and Measurement Clearinghouse.

Telch, M., Shermis, M. D., & Lucas, J. (1989). Anxiety sensitivity: Unitary personality trait or domain-specific appraisals? *Journal of Anxiety Disorders, 3*, 25-32.

Tobin, K. G., & Capie, W. (1979). *Test of Logical Thinking*. Athens, GA: University of Georgia.

Tufte, E. R. (1983). *The visual display of quantitative information*. Cheshire, CT: Graphics Press.

Veldman, D. (1989). *Pandora*. Austin, TX: The University of Texas at Austin.

Wyss, C. (1984). Planning a computerized measurement system. *Byte, 9*(4), 114-123.

Zuboff, S. (1986). *In the age of the smart machine: The future of work and power*. New York: Basic Books.

# Glossary*

**Algorithm.** A prescribed set of well-defined, unambiguous rules or processes for the solution of a problem in a finite number of steps; for example, a full statement of an arithmetic procedure for evaluating cosine $x$ to a stated precision. A computer can carry out the steps in many different types of algorithms. Thus, the study of computers and the study of algorithms are closely related subjects.

**ANSI  (American National Standards Institute).** An organization that acts as a national clearinghouse and coordinator for voluntary standards in the United States.

**Archive.**  (1) To copy programs and data onto an auxiliary storage medium, such as a disk or tape, for long-term retention. (2) To store data for anticipated normal long-term use.

**ASCII.**  Acronym for American Standard Code for Information Interchange, a 7-bit standard code adopted to facilitate the interchange of data among various types of data processing and data communications equipment.

**Asynchronous.**  Pertains to a mode of data communications that provides a variable time interval between characters during transmission.

**Batch.**  A group of records or programs that is considered a single unit for processing on a computer.

*Some terms taken from Webster's New World Dictionary of Computer Terms (3d ed.). Reprinted courtesy of Simon & Schuster.

**Batch processing.** (1) A technique by which programs to be executed are coded and collected together for processing in groups or batches. The user gives the job to a computer center, where it is put into a batch of programs, processed, and returned. The user has no direct access to the machine. (2) Processing as a group data that has been accumulated over a period of time or must be done periodically, as in payroll and billing applications.

**Baud.** A unit for measuring data transmission speed. One baud is 1 bit per second. Since a single character requires approximately 8 bits to represent it, the baud rate is divided by 8 to calculate the characters per second (cps) to be transmitted. For example, 300 baud equal 37.5 cps, 1200 baud equal 150 cps, 2400 baud equal 300 cps. Most commercial information services (CompuServe, The Source, and Dow Jones News/Retrieval) offer 300, 1200, and 2400 baud. Sometimes abbreviated as b.

**Binary.** Pertains to the number system with a radix of 2, or to a characteristic or property involving a choice or condition in which there are exactly two possibilities.

**Bit.** A binary digit; a digit (1 or 0) in the representation of a number in binary notation. The smallest unit of information recognized by a computer and its associated equipment. Several bits make up a byte, or a computer word.

**Bit map.** (1) An area in the computer's storage reserved for graphics. The bit map holds the picture that is continuously transmitted to the display screen. (2) An array of bits whose on/off status corresponds to the status of an array of other data.

**Boolean operator.** A logic operator, each of whose operands and whose result has one of two values.

**Branch.** The selection of one or more possible paths in the flow of control, based on some criterion. A programming instruction that causes transfer of control to another program sequence.

**Bug.** A term used to denote a mistake in a computer program or system or a malfunction in a computer hardware component. Hence, to *debug* means to remove mistakes and correct malfunctions.

**Byte.** (1) A grouping of adjacent binary digits operated on by the computer as a unit. The most common size byte contains 8 binary digits. (2) A group of binary digits used to encode a single character. Sometimes abbreviated b.

**Calculator.** Any mechanical or electronic machine used for performing calculations. Calculators, as distinguished from computers, usually require frequent human intervention.

**Card reader.** A machine that translates symbols coded on punched cards into electrical signals to send to a computer.

**Catalog.** (1) An ordered compilation of item descriptions and sufficient information to afford access to the items, such as a listing of programs or data file names that are stored on a floppy disk. To catalog a disk is to instruct the computer to print out a list of all of the files on the disk. (2) To so enter information into a table.

**CD-ROM.** A read-only optical storage technology that utilizes compact disks. *See also* ROM.

**Chip.** A small component that contains a large amount of electronic circuitry. A thin silicon wafer on which electronic components are deposited in the form of integrated circuits. Chips are the building blocks of a computer and perform various functions, such as doing arithmetic, serving as the computer's memory, or controlling other chips.

**Circuit.** (1) A pathway designed for the controlled flow of electrons. (2) A system of conductors and related electrical elements through which electrical currents flow. (3) A communication link between two or more points.

**Clone.** In non-biological terms, a product or idea that is an exact duplicate or copy of another.

**CMS.** Abbreviation for Conversational Monitor System, an operating system for IBM mainframe computers.

**COBOL.** Acronym for COmmon Business Oriented Language, a high-level language developed for business data processing applications. Every COBOL source program has four divisions: (1) Identification Division identifies the source program and output of a compilation; (2) Environment Division specifies those aspects of a data processing problem that are dependent upon the physical characteristics of a particular computer; (3) Data Division describes the data that the object program is to accept as input, create, or produce as output; and (4) Procedure Division specifies the procedures to be performed by the object program, using English-like statements.

**Code.** (1) A set of rules outlining the way in which data may be represented. (2) Rules used to convert data from one representation to another. (3) To write a program or routine (i.e., a programmer-generated code).

**Compatible.** A quality possessed by a computer system that enables it to handle both data and programs devised for some other type of computer system.

**Compile.** To prepare a machine language program (or a program expressed in symbolic coding) from a program written in a high-level programming language such as FORTRAN, COBOL, or Pascal.

**Component.** A basic part, an element; a part of a computer system; a portion of an application.

**CompuServe.** A major information service network, used by individuals as well as businesses, that features timely news features, stock market reports, electronic mail, educational programs, programming aids, and more. Personal computer owners can reference the CompuServe network via the common telephone system.

**Computer.** A device capable of solving problems or manipulating data by accepting data, performing prescribed operations (mathematical or logical) on the data, and supplying the results of these operations.

**Computer conferencing.** A system that enables people to conduct a conference, even when widely scattered geographically, by communicating through a computer network.

**Conversational.** Pertains to a program or a system that carries on a dialog with a terminal user, alternately accepting input and responding to the input quickly enough for the user to maintain his or her train of thought.

**Courseware.** The name given to computer programs written especially for educational applications, such as teaching reading, physics, art appreciation, arithmetic, German, or English skills.

**CPS.** Abbreviation for Characters Per Second, a unit for measuring the output of low-speed serial printers.

**CPU.** An abbreviation for Central Processing Unit. The component of a computer system with the circuitry to control the interpretation and execution of instructions. The CPU includes the arithmetic-logic unit and control unit.

**CR.** Abbreviation for Carriage Return, the operation of a character printer that causes the next character to be printed at the left margin.

**Cursor.** (1) A moving, sliding, or blinking symbol on a CRT screen that indicates where the next character will appear. (2) A position indicator used on a video display terminal to indicate a character to be corrected or a position in which data is to be entered.

**Data.** A formalized representation of facts or concepts suitable for communication, interpretation, or processing by people or by automatic means. The raw material of information. Individual pieces of quantitative information, such as dollar sales of carpets, numbers of building permits issued, or units of raw material on hand. Historically considered to be plural form of *datum*, but generally considered singular in data processing lexicon.

**Data collection.** (1) The gathering of source data to be entered into a data processing system. (2) The act of bringing data from one or more points to a central point.

**Data entry.** The process of converting data into a form suitable for entry into a computer system, such as by keying from a keyboard onto magnetic disks.

**Data management.** (1) A general term that collectively describes those functions of a system that provide access to hardware, enforce data storage conventions, and regulate the use of input/output devices. (2) A major function of operating systems that involves organizing, cataloging, locating, retrieving, storing, and maintaining data.

**Data processing.** (1) One or more operations performed on data to achieve a desired objective. (2) The functions of a computer center. (3) A term used in reference to operations performed by data processing equipment. (4) Operations performed on data to provide useful information to users.

**Database management.** A systematic approach to storing, updating, and retrieving information stored as data items, usually in the form of records in a file, by which many users, even at remote installations, can use common databases.

**DBMS.** Abbreviation for DataBase Management System, the collection of hardware and software that organizes and provides access to a database. The system provides the mechanisms needed to create a computerized database file, to add data to the file, to alter data in the file, to organize data within the file, to search for data in the file, and otherwise manage the data.

**Debug.** To detect, locate, and remove all mistakes in a computer program and any malfunctions in the computing system itself. Synonomous with *troubleshoot*.

**Delete.** To remove or eliminate; to erase data from a field or to eliminate a record from a file. A method of erasing data.

**Desktop computer.** A microcomputer. A complete computer system, designed to fit on the top of a desk, containing a microprocessor, input and output devices, and storage, usually in one box or package.

**Desktop publishing program.** An application program that permits the use of a microcomputer and a high-quality printer to produce reports, newsletters, brochures, magazines, books, and other publications.

**Device.** (1) A mechanical or electrical apparatus with a specific purpose. (2) A computer peripheral. (3) Any piece of physical equipment within or attached to a computer.

**Disk.**  A magnetic device for storing information and programs accessible by a computer. A disk can be either a rigid platter (hard disk) or a sheet of flexible plastic (floppy disk).

**Diskette.**  A floppy disk. A low-cost, bulk-storage medium for microcomputers and minicomputers.

**DOS.**  Acronym for Disk Operating System, a specialized, disk-oriented program that provides an easy-to-use link between the user and a computer's disk drive.

**Download.**  The process of transferring data from a large central computer to a smaller, remote computer system. Opposite of upload.

**Duplicate.**  To copy so that the results remain in the same physical form as the source; for example, to make a new diskette with the same information and in the same format as an original diskette.

**Edit.**  (1) To check the correctness of data. (2) To change the form of data as necessary by adding or deleting certain characters;  for example, adding special symbols and spaces, deleting nonsignificant zeros, and so on.

**Embedded command.**  In word processing, one or more characters inserted into the text that do not print but direct the word processing program or printer to perform some task, such as end a page or skip a line.

**Emulate.**  (1) To pattern one hardware system after another by means of an electronic attachment. The emulating system accepts the same data, executes the same programs, and achieves the same results as the emulated system. (2) To have a software program or hardware product simulate the function of another.

**Encode.**  To convert data into a code form that is acceptable to some piece of computer equipment.

**Encryption.**  The coding of data in such a way as to make it unintelligible without the key to decryption.

**Error checking.**  (1) Various techniques that test for the valid condition of data. (2) The process by which two telecommunicating computers can verify that the data received was error free.

**Export.**  For a database system, to send data out (usually to a disk file) in a form that other programs can use. Many database programs store their data in some coded form, but will export ASCII (text) files that can be read and edited with a normal text editor. Opposite of *import*.

**Feedback.**  (1) Any process whereby output from a sequential task serves to modify subsequent tasks. (2) A means of automatic control in which the actual state of a process is measured and used to obtain a quantity that modifies the input in order to initiate the activity of the control system. In data processing, information arising from a particular stage of processing could provide feedback to affect the processing of subsequent data; for example, the fact that an area of storage was nearly full might either delay the acceptance of more data or divert it to some other storage area.

**Field.** A single piece of information, the smallest unit normally manipulated by a database management system; for example a person's address in a personnel file. One or more fields compose a *record*.

**File.** A collection of related records treated as a basic unit of storage.

**Floppy disk.** A flexible disk (diskette) of oxide-coated mylar encased in a paper or plastic jacket that is used widely with microcomputers and minicomputers to provide storage at relatively low cost. Floppy disks come in three popular sizes: diameters of 8 inches (20.32 cm), 5 1/4 inches (13.3 cm), and 3 1/2 inches (9cm).

**Font.** A complete collection of letters, numbers, punctuation marks, and special characters of a consistent and identifiable size, posture, and weight. The term is often used to refer to typefaces or font families (e.g., Helvetica).

**Format.** (1) The specific arrangement of data. (2) The programming associated with setting up text arrangements for output. (3) Any method of arranging information that is to be stored or displayed.

**FORTRAN.** Acronym for FORmula TRANslator, a widely used high-level programming language used to perform mathematical, scientific, and engineering computations. FORTRAN has been approved as an American Standard programming language in two versions, FORTRAN and Basic FORTRAN.

**Full duplex.** Pertains to the simultaneous, independent transmission of data in both directions over a communications link. Contrast with *half duplex*.

**Gantt chart.** A time-based bar, line, or arrow chart depicting start and end points of activities or tasks, commonly used to depict scheduled deadlines and milestones for a project. Named after its developer, Henry Gantt.

**GIGO.** Acronym for Garbage In, Garbage Out, meaning that if the data input into a computer system is bad (Garbage In), then the data output from the system will also be bad (Garbage Out).

**Graph.** A diagram showing the relationship of two or more variable quantities. Sometimes called a chart.

**Half duplex** Pertains to transmission of data over a communications link that can occur in either direction but only one way at a time. Contrast with *full duplex*.

**Hard copy.** (1) A printed copy of machine output in readable form; such as reports, listings, or graphic images. (2) A photograph or transparency file of an image displayed on a visual display screen.

**Hard disk.** A fast auxiliary storage device that is mounted either permanently inside a computer or perhipherally in its own case. A single hard disk has storage capacity of several million characters or bytes of information.

**Hard wired.** Pertains to the physical connection of two pieces of electronic equipment by means of a cable.

**Heuristic.** Descriptive of an exploratory method of attacking a problem wherein the solution is obtained by successive evaluations of the progress towards the final results. From the Greek word *Eureka*, pertaining to the use of empirical knowledge to aid in discovery. Contrast with *algorithm*.

**Home.** The starting position for the cursor on a terminal screen, usually the top left-hand corner.

**Host computer.** (1) The central processing unit (CPU) that provides the computing power for terminals and peripheral devices connected to it. (2) The computer that is in charge during a telecommunications or local area network session. (3) The central, controlling computer in a network of computers.

**Hypercard™.** A kind of programming environment that organizes data into a form that emulates stacks of index cards, which the user then manipulates to create applications.

**Hypermedia.** Nonlinear branching databases that combine written, aural, and visual materials.

**Hz.** Abbreviation for Hertz, the international unit of frequency equal to one cycle per second.

**IBM Personal Computer™.** The first microcomputer family manufactured by the IBM Corporation and the most popular microcomputer to date. The IBM PC follows a modular design philosophy and consists of a computer processor, keyboard, and monitor. Other components may be added, such as a disk drive. The three members of this family of computers are the IBM PC™, IBM PC-XT™, and IBM PC-AT™.

**IBM Personal System/2™.** The next generation of microcomputer systems manufactured by the IBM Corporation after the IBM PC, offering considerably greater speed and sophistication.

**Image.** (1) An exact, logical duplicate stored in a different medium, e.g., the contents of computer memory displayed on a screen. (2) In computer graphics, the output form of graphics data, e.g., a drawn representation of a graphics file.

**Import.** To send data from a program to a database system. Opposite of *export*.

**Index.** (1) A symbol or number used to identify a particular quantity in an array of similar quantities; for example, X(5) is the fifth item in the array of Xs. (2) A table of reference, held in storage in some sequence, that may be accessed to obtain the addresses of other item of data, such as items in a graphics or data file.

**Informating.** The process of automating jobs or functions formerly performed manually, for example, the UPC or "bar codes" on supermarket products used for recording prices and maintaining inventory.

**Input.** (1) To transfer data from an auxiliary storage device into a computer's main storage unit. (2) The data a computer takes in. Contrast with *output*.

**Integrate.** The process of putting various components together to form a harmonious computer system.

**Integrity.** The capacity of programs or data to be used for their intended purpose.

**Interface.** A point or means of interaction between a computer and an external entity, whether operator, peripheral device, a communications medium. May be physical as in a connector, or logical as in a software program.

**Job.** A collection of specified tasks constituting a unit of work for a computer, such as a program or related group of programs processed as a unit.

**Keyboard.** An input device used to key programs and data into the computer's storage.

**Keypad.** An input device that uses a set of decimal digit keys (0-9) and special function keys. Can be a separate device or located on the right side of a standard keyboard.

**Kilobyte.** Unit of measure comprising 1024 bytes, commonly abbreviated K and used as a suffix describing memory size, e.g., a 24K system contains $24 \times 1024 = 24,576$ bytes of memory.

**Language.** A set of rules, representations, and conventions used to convey information.

**Laptop computer.** A notebook- or briefcase-size portable computer, usually weighing less than 10 pounds.

**Laser printer.** A nonimpact printing device that places images on a rotating drum using a laser beam. The drum places toner powder on those areas exposed to the laser, which are then fused into the paper to form characters.

**LaserWriter™.** A laser printer marketed by Apple Computer, Inc.

**Layout.** The overall design or plan, such as system flowcharts, schematics, diagrams, format for printer output, and makeup of a document or book.

**LCD.** Abbreviation for Liquid Crystal Display, whereby images are generated by reflecting light on a special crystalline substance. An LCD requires high illumination levels; display is invisible at low illumination levels. Because of its thin profile, LCD technology is often used in pocket calculators, pocket computers, laptop computers, keyboards, and other devices.

**LED.** Abbreviation for Light Emitting Diode, a commonly used alphanumeric display unit that glows when supplied with a specified voltage.

**Library.** A published collection of programs, routines, and subroutines available to every user of the computer. Also called *program library*.

**List.** (1) An ordered set of items. (2) Organization of data using indexes and pointers to allow for nonsequential retrieval. (3) To print every relevant item of input data. (4) A command to print program statements; for example, the LIST command in the BASIC language causes the system to print a program listing.

**Log.** A record of operations of a computer system listing each job or run, the time it required, operator actions, and other pertinent data.

**Lookup.** A procedure for using a known value to locate an unknown value in a table. Also called *table lookup*.

**Machine independent.** (1) Refers to the ability to run a program on computers made by different manufacturers or on various machines made by the same manufacturer. (1) Refers to a language or program developed in terms of the problem rather than in terms of the characteristics of the computer system.

**Macintosh™.** A popular microcomputer system manufactured by Apple Computer, Inc., considered the trendsetter in conventions for how a computer and its software should interact with the user. Some Macintosh innovations are now standard tools of the trade, such as the computer "mouse" for moving the cursor around the screen, "windows" for displaying various applications at once, and "icons" for indicating a tool or function with a picture instead of words.

**Macro.** A single, symbolic programming-language statement that, when translated, results in a series of machine-language statements.

**Mainframe.** The largest, fastest, and most expensive class of computers, used primarily by large organizations. Originally, the term referred to the extensive array of large rack-and-panel cabinets that held thousands of vacuum tubes in early computers. Mainframes have extremely high data-handling capacities and can occupy an entire room. *Supercomputers* are the largest, fastest and most expensive of the mainframes.

**Mark sensing.** The ability to mark cards or pages with a pencil to be read directly into the computer via a mark sense reader.

**Media.** The plural form of medium. In data processing, media can be classified as source (e.g., documents), input (e.g., diskettes), and output (e.g., magnetic tape and paper printouts).

**Megabyte.** 1,048,576 bytes or 1024 kilobytes; roughly one million bytes or one thousand kilobytes.

**Menu.** An on-screen list of options from which the user chooses a part of the program with which to interact, for example, to print a report or load a specific program stored on a disk. Menus enable computer users to use programs without knowing any technical methods.

**MHz.** Abbreviation for MegaHertz, one million cycles per second.

**Microcomputer.** The smallest and least expensive type of computer, in which microprocessors serve as the CPU. Commonly used in schools, businesses, and in the home as personal computers. Often referred to as *Micro.*

**Microprocessor.** The basic arithmetic, logic, and control elements required for processing, generally contained on one integrated circuit chip. Microprocessors are widely used as the control devices in microcomputers, household appliances, calculators and business machines, toys, video game machines, and thousands of other applications.

**Minicomputer.** A computer that is usually more powerful than a microcomputer, but less powerful than a mainframe computer.

**Modem.** Acronym for MOdulator/DEModulator, a device that provides communication capabilities between computer equipment over common telephone facilities. A modem translates digital pulses from a computer into analog signals for telephone transmission, and analog signals from the telephone into digital pulses the computer can understand.

**Mouse.** A device connected to a computer for the purpose of moving the cursor or other object around the display screen, typically a small box that, when moved around a flat surface, causes the cursor to move correspondingly around the screen. One or more buttons on the top of the mouse are used for specific actions. The mouse's main advantage is that it can move a cursor quickly and with great precision to any point on the screen, such as diagonally from one corner to another.

**Network.** (1) A system of interconnected computers and terminals. (2) A series of points connected by communications channels. (3) The structure of relationships among a project's activities, tasks, and events.

**OCR.** Abbreviation for Optical Character Recognition, whereby characters are printed in a type style that can be read by both machines and people.

**On-line.** (1) Equipment, devices, or persons being in direct communication with the central processing unit of a computer. (2) Equipment that is physically connected to the computer.

**Output.** Information that is delivered to the user as a result of computer processing.

**Peripheral equipment.** The input/output units and auxiliary storage units of a computer system, attached by cables to the central processing unit, used to input and output data and to store large amounts of data that cannot be held in the central processing unit at one time. Examples are graphics tablets, visual display terminals, and floppy disk drives.

**PERT.** Acronym for Program Evaluation and Review Technique, a management technique for control of large-scale, long-term projects. Involves analysis of the time frame required for each step in a process and the relationships of the completion of each step to the activities in succeeding steps.

**Pixel.** Shortened version of "picture element," the smallest unit of the display screen that can be stored, displayed, or addressed. The display screen is divided into rows and columns of tiny cells, each of which is a pixel. A computer picture is typically composed of a rectangular array of pixels, and the resolution of a picture is expressed by the number of pixels in the array. For example, a picture with $560 \times 720$ pixels is much sharper than a picture with $275 \times 400$ pixels.

**Plot.** To diagram, draw, or map with a plotter.

**Processor.** A device or system capable of performing operations upon data, such as a central processing unit (hardware) or compiler (software). A compiler is sometimes referred to as a *language processor.*

**Program.** A series of instructions that cause a computer to process data. Can be in a high-level source form, which requires intermediate processing before the computer can execute it, or in an object form that is directly executable by the computer.

**Protocols.** A set of rules or conventions governing the exchange of information between computer systems.

**Punched card.** A cardboard card used in data processing operations, in which tiny rectangular holes at hundreds of individual locations denote numerical values and alphabetical characters.

**Reader.** Any device capable of transcribing data from an input medium.

**Record.** A collection of related data treated as a unit to describe an item in a database. Each item is represented by a record that consists of one or more fields. For example, a personnel record would contain a "name" field and an "address" field.

**RGB video.** A form of color video signal distinctly different from the composite color video used in standard television sets in that images are displayed on a color monitor that has a separate electron gun for each color (e.g., red, green, blue), while ordinary color television uses only one gun. RGB monitors are noted for their crisp, bright colors and high resolution.

**ROM.** Abbreviation for Read Only Memory, a special type of computer memory that is permanently programmed with frequently used instructions, such as a BASIC language interpreter and operating system. Programs in ROM cannot be changed by the user, and remain in ROM when the computer is turned off. Several microcomputers use plug-in ROM modules that contain education, business, and games programs.

**Scanner.** An optical device that can recognize a specific set of visual symbols.

**Scripts.** Schema-like structures for representing sequences of events.

**Search.** To examine a set of items to identify those that have some desired property or predetermined criterion, such as a particular name or part number.

**Security.** The protection of hardware, software, or data against damage, theft, or corruption.

**Shareware.** Software that can be used and copied without charge. However, shareware is copyrighted and the copyright holder often asks that the user send a donation if the software is to be used regularly.

**Simulation.** (1) The modeling of a real problem by a computer. (2) The representation of certain features of the behavior of a physical or abstract system by the behavior of another system, such as the representation of physical phenomena by means of operations performed by a computer, or the representation of operations of a computer by those of another computer.

**Software.** Programs containing instructions that tell a computer what to do. Software may be built into the computer's ROM or may be loaded temporarily into the computer from a disk or tape. Contrast with *hardware.*

**Stack.** The program data file associated with HyperCard™ software.

**Stackware.** A type of software produced by the HyperCard™ program.

**Storage.** Descriptive of a device or medium that can accept and hold data for delivery on demand at a later time. The term is preferred over *memory.*

**Subprogram.** A segment of a program that performs a specific function, particularly useful when a specific function is required at more than one point in a program, in that the statements for that function can be coded once and executed at various points in the program.

**Subroutine.** A subsidiary routine which is executed only when called by some other program, usually the main program. Also called *subprogram.*

**Synchronous communications.** A method of exchanging data at very high speeds between computers, involving careful timing and special control codes.

**Telecommunications.** The transfer of data from one place to another over communications lines.

**Template.** (1) A plastic guide used in drawing geometric flowcharting symbols. (2) In computer graphics, the pattern of a standard, commonly used component or part that serves as a design aid. Once created, it can be subsequently traced instead of redrawn each time it is needed. (3) A set of instructions for relating information within a software development package, usually a spreadsheet. The template instructs the computer to perform certain operations on data contained within the spreadsheet, for example, to add 10 percent to shipping charges of those customers who live west of the Mississippi River. The template is stored on disk for future use.

**Terminal.** A keyboard/display or keyboard/printer device used to input programs and data to the computer and to receive output from the computer.

**Text editing.** A program used to manipulate text, for example, to erase, insert, change, and move words or groups of words. The text manipulated may be another computer program or any other arrangement of textual information.

**Time sharing.** A method of operation in which a computer facility is shared by several users for different purposes, apparently at the same time. The computer actually serves each user in sequence, but the high speed of the computer makes it appear that the users are being handled simultaneously.

**Transcribe.** To copy from one auxiliary storage medium to another. The process may involve conversion.

**Transfer rate.** The speed at which accessed data can be moved from one device to another.

**Translate.** To change data from one form of representation to another without significantly affecting the meaning.

**Troubleshoot.** A term applied to the task of finding and correcting a malfunction in a hardware unit or a mistake in a computer program. Synonymous with *debug*.

**UNIX.** An easy-to-use operating system developed by Ken Thompson, Dennis Ritchie, and coworkers at Bell Laboratories. Since the UNIX operating system is very easy to use, its design concept had great influence on operating systems for microcomputers. UNIX is widely used on a great variety of computers, from mainframes to microcomputers. It is a powerful operating system that has many high-level utility programs, and is capable of running a number of jobs at once. It has many applications, including office automation, network control, and control of numerically controlled machinery. Since it also has superior capabilities as a program development system, UNIX should become even more widely used in the future.

**UPC.** Abbreviation for Universal Product Code, developed by the supermarket industry for identifying products and manufacturers on product tags. A variety of manufacturers produce printers to print the 10-digit bar codes and optical scanning devices to read the codes during supermarket checkout.

**Update.** (1) To make data files more current by adding, changing, or deleting data. (2) To change a software system to reflect changes, new editions, or new information.

**Upgrade.** To reconfigure a computer system to increase its computing power.

**Upload.** To transfer data from a user's system to a remote computer system. Opposite of *download*.

**VAX.** A designation for large minicomputer systems manufactured by Digital Equipment Corporation.

**VLSI.** Abbreviation for Very Large Scale Integration, usually referring to chips that contain between 1,000 and 1 million components.

**VVLSI.** Abbreviation for Very Very Large Scale Integration, usually referring to chips that contain more than 1 million components.

**Window.** A portion of the video display area dedicated to some specific purpose. Special software allows the screen to be divided into multiple "windows" that can be moved around and made bigger or smaller. Windows allow the user to treat the computer display screen like a desktop in that various files can remain open simultaneously.

**Word processing.** A software system that enables the user to write, revise, manipulate, format, and print text for letters, reports, manuscripts, and other printed matter. Word processing is the most common use for personal computers in business and the home.

**Workstation.** A configuration of computer equipment designed for use by one person at a time. Can be a terminal connected to a computer or a stand-alone system with local processing capability, such as a graphics system and a word processor.

# Index

## DATE DUE